CHASING THE WHITE BLAZE

CHASING the WHITE BLAZE

THRU HIKING THE APPALACHIAN TRAIL

The Good Samaritan

Ron Knickrehm

RGK Wellness

Introduction

Introduction

The white blaze is the marker that is generally two inches wide by six inches long and is periodically painted on trees, rocks, posts, roads, guard rails, and other surfaces along the Appalachian trail. It helps to show you that you are actually on the Appalachian Trail without constantly looking at your map, app, or trail guide. When there are two blazes side by side with one lower than the other, it indicates a turn of the trail. If the higher blaze is on the right the trail turns to the right. If the higher blaze is on the left the trail turns to the left. The blue blaze, on the other hand, or any other color or shaped blaze for that matter, is a side trail or short cut or just another trail. When I would see the white blaze, I would feel confident that I was on the right path. However, when I wasn't paying attention and realized I hadn't seen one in a while, seeds of anxiety would creep into my mind. A debate would rage, at times, causing great angst. Do I just keep going or do I break out the map? Am I lost or just not paying attention? I have a rule: If you think you are lost, stop and go back to where you weren't lost and correct your path. It probably beats getting forever lost in the woods. The same holds true in life.

The White Blaze that marks the Appalachian Trail.

What would possess a person to write another book about hiking the Appalachian Trail? There are lots of books available to research in preparation for a thru hike or to just enjoy tails of the trail. One can live the AT adventure vicariously; but you just can't get enough of the adventure by just reading one or two books. I have read four books on the AT. Three of them were just for fun type reading and one was actually recommended for my preparation of the trek. My wife, on the other hand, checked out every book our library had about the trail and has read fifteen or so books and watched countless hours of video blogs. She has reported to me many of the details of others' experiences. Some of her reading placed an intense worst case possible scenario for disastrous hiking in the back of her mind, and she attempted to relay those to me as words of caution. The four books I read, along with my past hiking experience and a burning desire for this adventure fueled my drive to thru hike the Appalachian Trail in 2019.

I am not a writer and have poor typing skills so writing a book appears to be a daunting task. With the encouragement of my wife, daughters, friends, and others I have met along this journey, I will put down in words my experiences and some of the lessons I have learned so that others may enjoy the trail as I have. The book is not an exact chronology of events but I have used some events to illustrate lessons and perspectives I garnered for the trek. Some of my friends and acquaintances have told me they would never hike the trail but would like to live vicariously through my adventure. My hope is that you will enjoy the book. And those that want an adventure, I trust you can glean some valuable information from my ramblings to help you not only attain your goal to join the 2000 miler club but to enhance the adventure of a lifetime. It is better to learn from my mistakes and not experience them. It is less desirable to learn from your own mistakes but, by all means, learn from your mistakes as well.

This journey would barely be possible without the support and encouragement of my wonderful wife of forty-seven years. She would ask the hard questions about the details that I, in my enthusiasm, regularly overlooked. Some were impossible to answer while others were quite obvious once brought to my attention. She was able to hold down the home-front, send me mail drops of food, clothing, and equipment changes, and occasionally meet me for NNOTTs (nights not on the trail). She would be there for my trail family and was the best trail angel for many. She provided trail magic whenever she was near a trail head, which was often. Her trail name is Cutie Angel; many in my trail family called her Cutie, while others just called her Gail. Thank you for all that you have done to make this adventure possible.

This book will hopefully be a bit entertaining as well as informational as you start to plan your journey on the Appalachian Trail. The chronology of events is not totally exact as I have used some events to illustrate a particular lesson or experience. I do, however, try to convey the process that occurs over distance and time as accurately as I remember them. I hope you enjoy the process of planning your adventure as much as I enjoyed mine.

Contents

1

Preparing for the Hike

Can you really be totally ready to walk 2192 miles when the longest journey you have ever taken is about fifty miles at one time? The short answer is no, but you need to start somewhere. I have heard many times that the trail will train you so don't worry about getting in shape for it. It will train you, and you should hike under ten miles a day for a couple of weeks. In my first three weeks on the trail, I averaged sixteen miles each day.

While Tetiana and Anna were unable to be around to follow the hike they are avid hikers now.

Julia and Tetiana hike at a park in Maryland.

Anna intently listening to tales from the trail with her mom Katie.

Emma, Jacob, and Gail on our adventure to the Grand Canyon.

While some have done the hike with only a week or two of pre-thought, my journey started about twenty-five years ago. It was significantly fueled by a chance hike in Baxter State Park in Northern Maine in October of 2001. My wife and I had a long weekend trip planned to go to Acadia National Park in Maine to use up soon-to-expire frequent flyer miles. We flew into Portland, Maine, rented a car, and spent two days hiking around Acadia National Park enjoying the beautiful crisp fall weather. The first day we treated ourselves to lobster from Trenton Bridge Lobster where we selected our delicacy, and they cooked it to perfection. It was served wrapped in newspaper and placed in a paper bag to help retain the heat. On the way back to the hotel we bought a loaf of French bread and a bottle of wine, and this was our reward for the day's trekking. We were up early the next morning to watch the sun's rays first touch the Continental United States on Cadillac Mountain. While contemplating our trek down the mountain, we noticed a large cruise ship in the distance pulling into Bar Harbor. Later that morning the Park became extremely crowded. At that point we decided to evade the crowds to pile into our rental car and travel to Baxter State Park to climb Mount Katahdin. On our way, we purchased another lobster, bread, and wine and traveled to Millinocket, Maine. We stayed in a hotel outside the park. The next morning, we got up early ready to tackle a major hike. When traveling to the park, we missed its entrance and were delayed in getting to the ranger station to register to climb Katahdin. In hind sight, that was probably a good thing as it far more intense than we would have been prepared for. We did see our first two moose in the wild while we were lost and making incredible time. When we arrived at the park there were no more day hiker permits available, so we opted to hike south on the Appalachian Trail towards Abol Bridge. The weather was perfect, sunny and pleasantly cool. The fall leaves were gorgeous as we hiked along, and we could smell the amazing aroma of the hemlock fir trees. Brightly colored red and golden maple leaves flittered down onto the path and its surrounding forest to decorate the bright green fir trees in Christmas tree fashion. We ate lunch just above upper Abol Falls at a warm and sunny spot. Here is where the spark was ignited for a thru hike of the Appalachian Trail.

Once the spark was ignited, camping was just not the same. There was a longing for adventure every time we set out for car camping or actually looked out into the woods in our backyard. Backpacking is an extremely addicting activity and for me, that addiction has not abated in the least.

A few years later when a friend asked if I would be interested in backpacking the Knobstone Trail in southern Indiana, I jumped at the chance. How difficult could it be? It's not even fifty miles. (Only 48 miles.) After all, it is in Indiana. We are flatlanders here and corn fields abound. This escapade gave me a great experience that taught me many things. I learned the importance of knowing the difference between the elevation and the elevation change. In the forty-eight miles we hiked in three and a half days, I felt every inch of the 10,000 feet of elevation change. Were we really in Indiana? My forty-five pound pack was an added burden compared to my friend Jon's twenty-three pound pack. There are a few things I observed on that little hike. Sometimes you will get wet. There is nothing like the experience of icy spring water rushing into your boots when you slip and plunge your foot into a swollen creek, especially after you have been so careful not to get your feet wet. Get over it and get on with your hike. You won't melt. Trekking poles can not only reduce the swelling in your fingers by the end of the day but also add to your balance and help boost you over small creeks, logs, and other objects. Another benefit trekking poles provide is reducing the effects of sharp prickly things as well as some of the spiderwebs on the path when you are the first traveler on the trail in the morning. The comrade and friendships will endure like the smell of the campfires that are etched into my memories. I learned a lot on that hike and will continue to learn every time I am in the woods, not only about backpacking, but also about reconnecting and refreshing my soul.

With the knowledge of this experience, there was a lot of equipment to investigate and analyze for the next adventure. Other adventures included Manistee River Trail, the North Country Trail, the Grub Ridge Trail in winter and spring, the Jordan River Valley Pathway, and the Maryland section of the Appalachian Trail, to name just a few. The final push to thru hike, however, came with the solo SOBO (SOuthBOund) section hike of Maryland.

Julia and Caleb taking a break before I head south on the Maryland section.

Starting the hike in Pennsylvania with Gail, my three year-old grandson Caleb, my daughter and son-in-law is where the adventure began. My daughter, Julia, and I hiked the first half mile together to the park where we met Caleb, Jeff, and Gail. We hiked the next mile over four hours or so and intimately explored the trail from a three year-old's perspective. It was fascinating and a bit unnerving at times trying to corral Caleb from excursions into patches of poison ivy or from munching on a variety of colorful mushrooms and other non-edible foliage. It was a flat but grueling escapade into the wilderness. Stopping for lunch, we ate our peanut butter and jelly sandwiches, and I said my good-byes. I headed south while the rest of the crew headed back to Penn-Mar Park, the car, and eventually their home.

The trail quickly became quite rocky and difficult to follow as the trail was not well marked in that area. I was not used to the trail and that probably confounded my sense of direction as well. My first night brought me to designated camping where I would be one of the first to set up my tent and start cooking my dinner. After all of the stories I had heard about Appalachian Trail shelters, I thought I would avoid those for now. Not that I couldn't sleep with multiple people snoring and mice dancing on my sleeping bag, but I really wanted to avoid that experience at this point. There were several other campers that trickled into the area in groups of two or three. As my dinner was simmering, I noticed a young girl stopping at each group of campers, chatting for a moment and then moving on to the next group. I wondered what she was up to. I didn't have to wait too long before she came over to my campsite. In a thick Australian accent, she said "If you would like, you can come over by the fire and eat your dinner. There is a group of us that are thru hiking. We would love the company." I said, "I would enjoy that." I was a bit apprehensive but excited at the same time. I had an unopened bag of chocolate chips I brought along to satisfy my sweet tooth but decided to share those with the group of five thru hikers sitting around the fire. When I arrived at the fire pit, there was seating made out of stones that resembled crudely fashioned Adirondack chairs. I introduced myself as a south bound Maryland section hiker and announced that I had brought treats to share. One of the older gentlemen briskly exclaimed, "You brought cigarettes and beer?!" I said, "No, just some chocolate." He said, "Oh, that's good too." Little did I know at that moment, I was responsible for Trail Magic. As we ate, I asked each of the hikers what their trail names were and what brought them to the trail. The answers were very fascinating, which is why it is the topic of another chapter. It was great conversation as we passed around the chocolate chips, and I mostly listened to the stories of the trail. Their stories were intriguing. This was really a pivotal moment in driving my passion for backpacking.

The next morning, I packed up and headed south to the next camping destination which was the Ed Garvey Shelter about four miles from Harpers Ferry, West Virginia. I took in all of the historical sites, views, sounds, and smells of the green tunnel that is the Appalachian Trail traveling over South Mountain. I passed the War Correspondents' Memorial and the Washington Monument and took a quick tour of the South Mountain State Park Visitor Center. Arriving a bit later in the day, I found the shelter jam packed with section hikers, thru hikers, and a whole bunch of Boy Scouts. The Scouts were trying persistently but ineffectively to start a fire, the smoke burning their eyes and irritating most everyone else around them. I sat next to a thru hiker while preparing to cook my chicken and rice. As I ignited my Jet Boil, it roared for three or four seconds and then, POOF, it went out. I did not say a word but just sighed and thought, "Poor planning on my part. It looks like cold-soak crunchy chicken and rice for me. Cold soaking involves soaking your food cold over the course of the day so it is not so crunchy and somewhat edible. In this case it will be a really disgusting dinner." The thru hiker next to me looked over and asked, "Did you just run out of fuel?" I said, "Yeah, looks like cold-soak for me". He told me I had to use his fuel canister because he ran out the evening before last with the same dilemma, and his dinner was horrible. He had just resupplied last night in Harpers Ferry and had a full fuel canister. I was then the recipient of Trail Magic in the form of a hot dinner of chicken and rice. In gratitude, I shared the rest of my chocolate chips with the thru hiker.

After dinner, I helped the Boy Scouts invigorate the fire with my micro-bellows which impressed them and got the fire to grow with a lot less smoke. The microbellows is a small collapsible antenna looking device that allows you to blow on the embers of a fire to help get it started. More on that in chapter 11. After a little while at the fire with dusk approaching, I went to my tent to hit the sack. It was very warm so I lay atop my sleeping bag dozing off while recounting the day's hike in my head. I faintly heard a hiker walking into the camping area as it was getting dark. A short while later, a solo NOBO (NOrthBOund) girl set up her tent about fifteen feet from mine and had her dinner. She hit the sack as darkness fell upon the designated camping area. Shortly thereafter she began bouts of coughing, and it became pretty regular. This went on for about fifteen minutes when I remembered I had cough drops in my pack. I slipped on my shorts, dug out the half dozen cough drops I had and headed to my neighbor's tent. I said, "Excuse me ma'am, are you OK? I have some cough drops that have tea tree oil in them and that may help your cough." She said she had this cough only when she would lie down at night. She consented to try the cough drops but only wanted one. I told her I would be off the trail tomorrow and if they did not help, she could give them to another hiker in need. I also recommended that she seek medical attention at her next re-supply if she was not better. The coughing subsided and then stopped, and I presume we both slept well that evening. At least I slept well. Trail Magic. These experiences as a section hiker cemented my affinity to the Appalachian Trail.

In the process of physically preparing for the Trail, I continued to jog and hike regularly. I am a regular jogger so that part was easy. I run regularly with a group of runners. We are known as the OGRES which stands for Old Guys Running Every Sunday. Some members of our unofficial group have been running every Sunday morning for twenty five years. I have been in the group for about fifteen years. We also try to run a 5K called "Fitness Friday" every Friday in the summer as well as several local races just for fun and a little exercise.

Over the two years prior to the start of my hike, I invested in some key equipment upgrades. A 700 fill down sleeping bag from the REI Garage Sale, some lightweight clothing, an AWOL Miller Appalachian Trail guide, a battery pack for my phone, and a variety of other small items I thought necessary. Some of the items came from the Cairn subscription where we received a variety of backpacking items in the mail to trial and review. My wife and I would always open it together. It was like Christmas for hikers once a month!

The fall before I was to start, I decided to test out my gear choices by doing a solo yoyo (out and back) hike on the Knobstone Trail. I did a night hike of about three miles on a clear and cool night that tested my headlamp. A huge raccoon scared the bejesus out of me as it ran across the trail not more than an arm's length in front of me. So far so good. I discovered I was in pretty good physical shape but was running out of batteries in my phone. The battery I brought was only good for one charge. The next day I hiked about sixteen miles and, in the evening, it started to rain lightly. That night, it rained torrentially, and my phone died due to the short battery life. My wife told me she would call for a search party if I didn't let her know each day that I was okay. We hadn't anticipated that my battery wouldn't last long enough to do so. I also found out that my fifteen year old tent leaked like a sieve, and my boots were in pretty bad shape. The hike went quickly from a 100 mile hike yoyo to a solo sprint back to the car the next day to recharge and re-evaluate. It turned out to be a thirty mile out and back. Good choice as I did not want the search party out for me. After some research, I purchased an Ankor 10,000 W battery and Oboz Bridger hiking boots which have both served me very well.

When deciding on a tent, Gail and I stopped at an REI store in Madison, Wisconsin when returning from a trip there. At the store, we set up a multitude of tents and climbed in to test them out. I was torn between one I really liked and one that was a lot less expensive. Gail looked at me and said, "My goodness, this is going to be your home for six months! For crying out loud! Spend the money!" Thank you, sweetie. I have really enjoyed the larger tent which only added about fourteen ounces. It is good to spread out and have all my gear, minus the bear canister, inside and out of the rain and dew. I will chat more about tent choices later in the equipment chapter.

It was recommended that I read a few books to prepare. I have read *A Walk in the Woods, As Far As the Eye Can See,* and *Hiking Through* with the last two being insightful and entertaining. The one book that was not the most entertaining but was one of the most helpful, was *Appalachian Trials.* There were three important recommendations I gleaned from that book. The first was that you do not have to accept the first trail name you are given. I chose the first one given to me as it seemed appropriate. Another was that you should not become a part of a trail family that is toxic to you or that does not fit your hiking style. You really must hike your own hike. You can either hike a bit faster and farther to avoid a particular group or take a zero or two to let them travel ahead. Hike your own hike. Otherwise you will be miserable, and that is not why you are there. The third piece of advice that was helpful was to tell everyone you know and even those you don't that you are hiking the whole thing and when you are going to start. That way when you are having a bad day and want to quit or things just get hard, you will not want to let all those people down and will be apt to continue on your hike. There were many days when it had rained for several days and I was tired, wet, cold and hungry, when I had to tell myself, "Just keep walking. You don't want to let people down." Not to say that breaking a leg or a family emergency couldn't take you off the trail, but, at least you won't leave without a really good reason. I would have left the trail in a heartbeat for my family.

The rest of the prep was making the home front ready for my six month absence and the logistics of hiking supplies, equipment, and other sundry needs I may have on the trail. That included probable food mail drops and equipment and clothing changes. This was based on my thoughts and research with the help of Gail. This last part of the prep was one of the most frustrating and stressful parts. More on that later.

We decided to purchase a van that I would customize to act as a support vehicle that would allow Gail to follow and support my travels along the trail. We named the van Tiny. We had the inverter, solar panels, roof vent, batteries, and shore station installed by a professional, and we thank Elite Van Conversions in Elkhart, Indiana, for their expertise in this area. I built a cabinet with a drawer over the inverter and added overhead shelves. We purchased and I installed a swivel to the passenger's front seat to allow more seating as well. We also purchased some high-tech super insulation for the floor, walls, and ceiling that was very helpful in controlling temperature changes in that large tin can Gail called home when she was on the road. That helped a bit so we didn't feel like we were staying in an oven or an ice box. Gail worked tirelessly to get insulated window covers, pillows, curtains, and other things we thought we would need to travel safely. It was an intense scramble to get Tiny livable before our departure date. Here again, Gail viewed countless hours of MyVanLife video blogs to help her navigate the details of a lone female living out of a van in strange places. I believe she is now a certified solo van lifer female. I think a lot of our family thought we were just plain nuts.

My grandchildren would track my progress along the route and mark a map of the trail. My granddaughter, Emma and her younger brother Eli would keep track of my progress with on a long trail map that was hung in their dining room. I was fortunate to occasionally have cell coverage and speak with Eli who would ask amazing questions about the adventure. My daughter Katie sent a picture of my three-year-old grandson Titus, who was ready to join the adventure with his backpack on and map in hand. I am sure that Anna, who was less than a year old, was cheering for me as well.

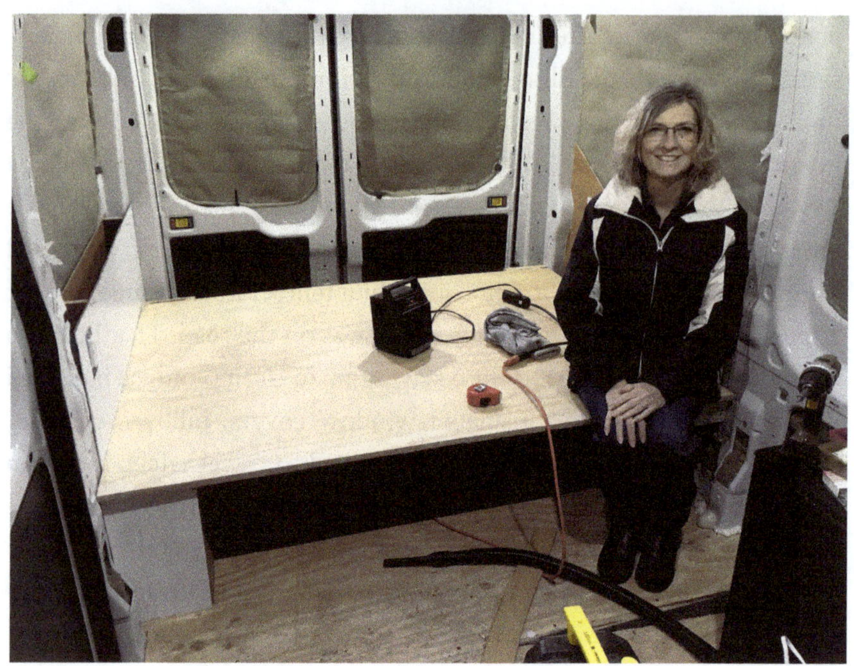

Gail checks out the height of the bed in Tiny.

Grandsons, Titus and Owen check to see where they can hide in Tiny to tag along.

Daughters Laura and Katie point the way to make sure I know what signs to look for on my way.

Grandson Titus is dressed and ready to join the adventure with pack and map in hand.

Grandson Eli tracks my progress daily on his full length map of the trail.

2

What or Who Drives to the Trail

(Literally or Figuratively)

My Maryland section hike several years ago, that I mentioned previously, allowed me to chat with five thru hikers by the fire while we ate dinner. I was very welcomed and asked each hiker what their trail name was and what had brought them to the trail. The stories varied. One person I judged to be in his early thirties was just released from military service and appeared to be suffering from PTSD. He said he was just out on the trail to get his head back together but the thru hikers were encouraging him to stay for the entire journey with them. He sported some military gear and was using a cheap blue tarp as a type of bivey. A bivey is a basic shelter that can keep the rain off and give you a modest bit of protection from the cold ground. As we were speaking around the fire, I leaned forward to pass the chocolate chips and noticed a rather large snake slithering behind the pile of rocks I was sitting on. There was some excitement and a discussion about how the bivey may not provide much protection from critters. The very fit young lady in her late twenties from Australia was there because she was between job assignments as an outdoor adventure guide. She had enough money set aside for the adventure and already had most of the equipment she would need. She had time, money, and a passion for adventure, so this was just the trail for her. One guy just fed up with his job and his boss had enough saved for an adventure. Because he had an issue with his boss, he just did not show up one day and headed out to the trail. He really didn't like the line of work he was in and planned on changing careers after he returned from his hike. Another man had recently retired from the military and decided this was something he had always wanted to do, and this was his opportunity. The final gentleman was divorced and had sold a business, started another and then sold it. The last business had a non-compete clause and, as money was no object, he decided that a thru hike would be a great adventure to take up some of his spare time and get away from his ex-wife. This appeared to be a trail family as they traveled together and knew each other pretty well. More on trail families later.

I continued to ask the same question during my thru hike with some variation. The people I traveled with, my trail family, had a variety of reasons for being on the trail. The original trail family I belonged to were three other individuals that were totally different. The family consisted of Nathan, later known as Classic, Jesse who was Flamingo, Jennifer who was called Balto. I was called the Good Samaritan. I will start with Flamingo as he was the youngest at about twenty-four years old. He was from Maine and had graduated from college with a degree in mechanical engineering. Instead of getting a job in his degree, he decided to strike out with the Peace Corp and taught high school math and science in Africa. After completing his two-year commitment, he had money in the bank and was not ready to start a regular job. He was single with no commitments and no bills so why not do a thru hike? After all, he was from Maine and could just walk home. The other gentleman was a brilliant thirty-nine year old prosecuting attorney who had just lost his job. He thought he really wanted to get away from people and figure life out. The third person in our family was an outdoor adventure junkie. She was retired, I think, and had rental properties in Alaska that supported her adventures. She regularly spent winters in exotic destinations hiking and retreating from the cold. One of her favorite things, however, was to backpack and ski on glaciers. I have skied on a glacier before and, even as a young guy, I thought that was crazy. As far as age, "You don't ask a lady that question!" Just let me say she looked to be in her late twenties.

Left to right, myself, Flamingo, Classic, and Balto in Erwin Tennessee.

My trail family grew and shrank as the trail is a linear community and relationships are quite fluid. You may hike with someone for a day and not see them for two weeks or more and then hike with them for two more weeks later on down the trail. Many of the trail family I traveled with were students with time and available funds between semesters or just young and looking for their calling in life. One young man, trail named Frosting, worked and saved enough money to enable him to hike. When he was done hiking, he went back to work and save enough to return to hiking. There was a medical student, Starfish, from Germany; a recent graduate from a school in Germany, Snow White; a student majoring in physics, Physics; an outdoors engagement student, Comet; and a variety of others backpacking to find adventure and for the love of the outdoors. People come to the trail for a variety of reasons.

Some people come to the trail just for the sake of the challenge and adventure. As an old guy, I fit into that category quite nicely. Some of our younger trail family did as well.

The trail can be an extremely harsh and demanding environment and monumentally challenging. At the same time, it can be a very healing experience. Countless souls have come to the trail for solitude and self-reflection and to get away from people, but in reality, many times they find lasting relationships, self-worth, and healing. They find a sense of who they are and learn to be themselves. Because on the trail, there is no personal history unless you share it. Generally, the hikers will accept you for who you are and will not be judgmental. Some hikers find they don't like the person they have become and turn out to be more connected to the person they truly are. Sometimes a complete stranger is able to ask hard questions without judgement which can help us to look inside to see flaws we should probably work on. Other times a trail family can speak truth to us about our strengths that we just can't see. I have seen hikers find inner strength they did not know they were capable of to get through tough parts of the trail physically and mentally. Thru hikers spend endless hours with that one person that gives us the most trouble, ourselves.

Classic found friendships that will last a lifetime. He was able to renew his belief in humanity. I think his foul language improved a little as well.

I had a conversation with someone that had an interesting perspective about some of the older hikers on the trail and older men in general, meaning those that are over fifty years or retired. He also said this would apply to men in general from his acquaintances. He said that men who are not satisfied sexually in their relationship will do one of about five things;

1. They will have an affair, sometimes with a younger woman but not always. Some are not thin, attractive, intellectual, athletic

or a good conversationalist, just available and willing and enjoy the attention. They will give up everything without thinking just to have a relationship they think is better. Many times, it can be much worse and make their life more miserable than it was before.

2. They will become addicted to pornography to fill the void of intimacy. This is a hollow substitute and never fulfills the need. It directly and indirectly supports the sex trafficking trade. It is also destructive to all other relationships making intimacy with another almost impossible and rarely meaningful.
3. They will start drinking to the point of becoming alcoholic or at least drink heavily and often. This substitute can not only have severe legal and financial consequences; this behavior is also destructive to relationships as well.
4. They will join a fraternity and do crazy stuff with a bunch of guys and occasionally it will involve heavy drinking as well. Many times, they will have an exclusive mancave with man-stuff for their new or old friends that may be in the same situation. Not all man caves fit this category so I am not being judgmental of man caves. They do have a good purpose.
5. The other alternative is to have one or even many wild and crazy adventures. Some escapades will require great physical strength, endurance, and commitment. Some are also just really, really expensive. So, in the case of this reason, their spouses may drive them to the trail literally and figuratively.

Just to set the record straight, my wife drove me to the trail literally but not figuratively. She is an amazing woman, and as I have said previously this would not have been possible without her support. She not only dropped me off, she also supported me along the way.

3

Start Your Hike

When you start a journey that is 2,192 miles long and the longest backpacking journey you have taken is just under fifty miles, there is a fairly steep learning curve. Kind of like the steepness of some of your climbs on the trail. When asked by my oldest daughter, Laura, if I would write a journal, I was very hesitant. Writing is very time consuming and can be difficult in cold and wet weather conditions and when you are probably exhausted and hungry and just want to hit the sack. Not to mention that paper is heavy and pens don't work when wet or when it is dark or you are tired. Excuses, excuses, excuses! When my daughter asked me that question a couple of weeks the Christmas before the hiking adventure began, I did not think much of it. For Christmas in 2018, I received the usual gifts related to hiking but was surprised to find one I had not expected from my daughter. It was a voice recorder. She relayed to me that when she was in middle school, she would walk the two blocks from her school to my office so she could ride home with me and not have to ride the bus. She would sit under my desk and do homework and study. She remembered that at the end of my day treating patients as a physical therapist, I would get back to my desk and dictate notes. That was a fond memory for her and she thought I could do the same for my hiking journal. The recorder weighed about 2 ounces with batteries and an SD card. I could protect it from the elements in the water tight bag with my phone and other electronics. It did not take a lot of time to figure out how to use, it even though it was not like the dictation system I had used previously. Through trial and error, I found it was a great way to journal, and it added sound effects to the trail conditions at the time. The sound of the wind, birds, and occasionally fellow hikers would add to my memory of the experience. I have over forty hours of ramblings in my audio journal. I would highly recommend this type of journaling, but a word of advice; figure out how to use the recorder before you strike out on the trail. It makes it a lot less stressful.

Starting the adventure, I found that my regular jogging and occasional trips on the Knobstone Trail in southern Indiana prepared me quite well for this adventure. In the first couple of hundred miles, I hiked quite a bit faster than many of my fellow hikers on the trail. Many hikers I only passed or spent only one night in a shelter with their company. There were a few exceptions and those hikers would become my trail family.

Gail and I started the adventure together leaving Indiana on February 23, 2019. We registered our hike on-line several weeks before as a thru hike for me and a section hike for Gail. I set a tentative plan for my first four nights, and Gail's hike would be an out and back overnight trip. I had no idea how far I would be able to hike so this was just a wild guess for me. When we arrived on February 25th , we attended the thru hiker orientation at Amicalola Falls State Park. We reviewed "Leave No Trace" principles. I re-learned how to dig a proper cat hole and bathroom etiquette in the woods as well as a few rules particular to the AT. At the orientation, we met a few fellow hikers, Hawk, Sarah Jane and a few others starting the thru hike for 2019. Sarah had a pack similar to mine, large and heavy. Hawk, on the other hand, had a pack that weighed twelve pounds. Hawk was going to attempt a yo-yo of the trail that year as he had thru hiked a couple of times in previous years. Gail and I planned to hike to the starting point on Springer Mountain via the Len Foote Trail and spend the night in the tent. This trail is longer than the normal route. The other access path is fewer miles to Springer, but you will climb 635 steps to the top of the falls. The two paths converge about 3.4 miles from Springer Mountain. The approach trail is not included in the actual trail mileage. In the morning, Gail would return to the van, and I would head north. I rearranged my pack and added more than enough food to last for a few days to include a sandwich for my lunch after Springer. We didn't leave too early and had lunch at the Len Foote Lodge as we took the longer path up to Springer Mountain. When we came to the main trail, we were surprised to meet Hawk and Sarah Jane who were hiking together. They had not known each other prior to meeting at registration. Hawk told us that he was taking it easy today and would put the hammer down tomorrow. We hiked significantly faster and made it to the shelter and tenting area and set up camp before they arrived. I set up our tent, reorganized our gear. We ventured back to the marker that indicated we were at Springer Mountain and took pictures of the start of this epic journey.

Gail and I at the summit of Springer Mountain which is the AT southern terminus.

By the time we made it back to the tent it was cold and dark-thirty (see Chapter 4) so we made dinner and hit the sack. We heard other hikers arrive and set up camp around us so we didn't sleep very soundly. Some of my restlessness was because it was very cold and the other was the anxiety of marching off into the wild unknown in the morning. During the night, I tried to nudge Gail frequently to roll over as she was breathing loudly. Some people call this snoring, but Gail doesn't snore! After three or four nudges, she became a bit irritated and asked, "What are you doing?" I said, "You were snoring, and I just wanted you to roll over." She retorted, "Do you hear me snoring now? Am I snoring now or is that a bear lying next to our tent?" It seems that one of the late arrivals for the evening pitched his tent only inches from ours, and he snored like a freight train. Sorry Gail!

As daylight began to illuminate the inside of the tent, Gail asked what was on the top of the tent. I had no clue but was sure it wasn't a leaf that had fallen because the trees were bare. Besides, the unidentified object was square. I put my frozen clothes on and ventured out to find I had left my sandwich on the top of the tent. I might as well have shouted, “Here, Bear! Here is a snack for the evening!” That did not instill confidence for Gail in my backpacking skill set. I made breakfast and filled our packs. I kissed Gail good-bye and, if all went well, I would see her at Neel Gap two days later.

Gail and I after registering for the start of our adventure.

In the evening on our way back to the van from our visit to the Outdoor Center, we met a limping middle-aged woman and her husband. I stopped to ask if she was section or thru hiking and if she would like me to check out her knee. I am the Good Samaritan after all and it is what I do. She moaned, “Not really, I am through hiking not thru hiking”. About twenty-five percent of thru hikers are through hiking at Neel Gap. There is a large old oak tree there that Is filled with pairs of shoes as many of the hikers tie their shoes together and chuck them up into the branches to say goodbye to the trail.

The hiking over the next few days was beautiful even though it was cold and rainy and occasionally frosty. The views of the oceans and rivers of fog in the mountains were amazing. The frost in the mornings felt like a multitude of fairies had worked overtime at warp speed to decorate the woods and the trial. They were shrouded in frost and ice that sparkled in the morning sunlight. On the trail, there was frost that seemed to sprout and grow up from the ground even on days that were relatively warm. It is known as hoarfrost. It was truly magical. Over the next six days of hiking, I averaged sixteen miles a day and enjoyed spectacular views as there were no leaves to block the sights. The wet weather provided frequent places to stop and filter water. In the past, I have filtered water from very shallow mud puddles. Not here though. There was an abundance of clear crisp cold spring water most of the way. Many of the springs were piped and you could have safely taken a drink without filtering. I always filtered my water just to be on the safe side. I learned quickly how heavy water is and planned to not carry more than necessary. It is easier to carry it on the inside than the outside. The tradeoff for the abundance of water, great views without leaves, and cold weather were temperatures dipping into the single digits, snow, and ice.

Gail spent several days visiting family nearby and one night in Helen, Georgia, while she waited to meet up with me at a trailhead. When speaking to the Chamber of Commerce she was informed that there was no overnight parking in the town, and they were not aware of safe places to park outside of town. They recommended speaking with someone from one of the local churches to see if they had any recommendations. When she spoke to someone from the local church, they invited her to the evening service with a pot luck dinner afterwards. The Bible study and singing were great and so was the dinner. They also arranged for a safe place to park close by. That made the day a lot less stressful.

I hiked sixteen miles to a trail head near Franklin, North Carolina, where I would depart the trail for a zero day with Gail in Tiny. About a mile from the trail head, I spotted a young lady hiking SOBO which made me ecstatic. It was Gail, and I would get to have a NNOTT, a zero, hot shower, hot food, clean clothes, and best of all hugs from my sweetheart: happy, happy me. While waiting for me at the trailhead, she met a lady named Brenda who was supporting her husband and son who were hiking the trail. Her husband was Smiles and her son was Tigger. She would wait at some of the trailheads with Gail, and they got to know each other a bit. Gail and Brenda's paths crossed several times over the next couple of weeks. They would call each other occasionally to keep track of where their hikers were and if they needed anything.

In Franklin, I was able to take a free hot shower at the Community Center. Gail was very good at investigating each town where we stayed. She contacted the Chamber of Commerce and let them know I was thru hiking. She would find out where we could park for the evening, if there was a laundry, a place to take a shower, what restaurants were in the area, and anything else that would be helpful to a weary hiker. The second night in Franklin, we ate at the Lazy Hiker Brew Company where I would meet most of the hikers in my extended trail family. I did not know that at the time, but we would become a family and we are truly close, even today. After Franklin, I would see Gail in three days at the Nantahala Outdoor Center (NOC). She got spooked by someone who was a little creepy parked at one of the trailheads. When she got to the NOC she relayed her experience to the outfitters there and asked if there was an out of the way place to park for the evening. She was directed to a back parking lot not open to the public and settled in for the night and waited for my arrival. Gail watched the kayakers paddle down the river adjacent to the restaurant while she waited, scoped out the local services, and tried to get the lay of the land in anticipation of my arrival. When I arrived, I resupplied and purchased a pair of gloves. Gail had OBOZ hiking boots that were irritating her foot and one of the salesmen showed her a way to tie her shoe that would relieve the pressure. It was like she had a new pair of shoes. The people there were great.

Gail ran into Brenda at the NOC. Brenda reported that her husband had injured his ankle, and they were going to spend the night at a motel in a nearby town and possibly see a doctor the next day. She asked if we had a place to stay. Gail said, "We always have a place. Even if it does not have heat at least it has a bed, and it is dry." Brenda offered to give us their bunk house room as they were not staying there and would not get a refund. It is warm and has the availability of a hot shower and laundry. She would not take money and told Gail to enjoy it. Gail thanked her and wished her well in town. It was a great respite after a couple of days of hiking in the cold rain. This was wonderful Trail Magic and much appreciated.

Wintry scene when hiking in North Georgia.

A frosty winter scene from Mount Albert.

Over the next week or so, our trail family would grow and coalesce into the group eventually known as the Frubble family. I had been hiking regularly with Balto, Nathan, and Flamingo. Balto was off the trail for at least ten days after our re-supply in Irwin, Tennessee, and I didn't know if she would be able to catch up to the trail family with that much time away. She did not return but did do an additional section after staying with a friend for a day or two. She told me she accidentally did a long thirty-mile day before heading for beach time in Hawaii. We are still friends and stay in contact.

Several other hikers that I had met several times on the trail were also at the iconic Overmountain Shelter when arrived on March 23rd. They included Snow White, Starfish, Legolas, Physics, and Frosting. Nathan had reiterated many times that he did not see any trail name that would fit him and was okay not having a trail name. While sitting around the campfire, the conversation turned to Nathan's lack of a trail name. He repeatedly refused to accept any of the myriad of suggestions until Starfish came up with Classic, reasoning that he enjoyed classical music and classical literature and was a lawyer. I don't know what the lawyer part had to do with it, but it must have been the key to swinging his acceptance of his new moniker. He was known as Classic from that point on. This was a great stay as there was Trail Magic of soda, beer, Ho Hos, and a variety of other snacks just before the shelter.

The Overmountain Shelter is a classic old red barn and somewhat in disrepair. It has been determined to be unsafe for habitation, and the repair cost is significant. It is scheduled to be condemned and demolished in 2020. I was fortunate to be one of the last groups of hikers to shelter there before it was razed.

Overmountain shelter looking from the end.

The lower sleeping section of Overmountain Shelter.

Fresh Ground providing Trail Magic near Glasgow Virginia. Frosting, Snow White, two section hikers, Flamingo, Fresh Ground, and Cutie Angel.

Gail would return to meet me at Glasgow on April 16th and follow me for five days before gathering me from the trail at the entrance to Shenandoah National Park on Good Friday of Easter weekend.

4

Terminology

If you hadn't already noticed in reading this book there is some terminology and acronyms that are somewhat strange. Hence this chapter. Hikers' conversation on the AT:

"Hey, are you a NOBO or SOBO? SOBO LASHER. How was Vermud with all the rain and treecipitation? I just did a thirty to get done with Rocksylvania but found a great Aycer for my zero with a NNOTT and have raging hiker hunger. You must have hiker legs too then."

The language is unique for the trail and can be a little confusing at times. It is filled with some abbreviations and slang but mostly acronyms. Knowing some of the essential basic abbreviations with Appalachian Trail hikers will reduce confusion and increase understanding when speaking with these adventurers. A **thru hiker** is one that plans to complete the entire trail from Georgia to Maine in one hiking season. A **section hiker** will hike a portion or section of the trail, and eventually attempt to hike the entire trail in sections over several years. A **LASHER** is a Long Ass Section Hiker, meaning taking many, many years. A **NOBO** starts at Springer Mountain in Amicalola Falls State Park in Georgia and goes north to Mount Katahdin in Baxter State Park in Maine. A **SOBO** starts at Mount Katahdin and ends at Springer Mountain.

The following is a list some of the most popular acronyms:

Purist:A hiker that, to the best of their ability, walks every inch of the trail. They do not bypass difficult parts or take short cut blue blazes. When they leave the trail to go to a shelter or to town for re-supply, they go back to that same spot to start hiking again. They want to see every single white blaze. I was a purist.

Flip Flopper: This is a hiker who starts somewhere in the middle of the trail and hikes to one end and then returns to go in the other direction to finish the trail. A Flip Flopper can always travel in one direction or may do different sections in different directions. No hard fast rules here. They just want to complete the hike in one calendar year.

Yellow striper: This hiker may hitchhike around difficult parts of the trail or get a ride to catch up to a trail family. This is acceptable as long as you don't try to lie about it. Scamper was a yellow striper and just enjoyed being on the trail with the trail family. If she would fall behind because she enjoyed a stay at a particular hostel or town, she would just hitch a ride to catch up. She also hiked barefoot a lot of the way in Vermud. Easier on the shoes, harder on the feet. She was truly a free spirit.

A twenty, a thirty, or any number after "a": This is the distance hiked in a day. I did many twenties and four thirties during my journey. Some hikers also will just inform others of the number. "I did a fourteen today and plan to do a twenty-three tomorrow." Some folks don't keep track well. Some folks lie.

Zero: That is a day where you do no hiking on the trail. Hence zero. These days can be a single day or even a couple of weeks. A zero of one or two days is used to re-supply, repair or replace gear, do laundry, rest, consume large quantities of calories, or just have a recuperation day and do something different. Longer zeros are meant for recovery from injury or pre planned events like graduations or weddings or other family or social obligations.

My first zero day was in Franklin, North Carolina. Gail had returned to the trail after visiting with a friend in Georgia for a few days and met me at a trail head in the evening with our van. She found out that we could park overnight at the Walmart or near the Franklin Community Center in a parking lot at a closed shopping center. She also discovered that I could take a free hot shower at the Community Center. If I had wanted to, I could play a pick-up basketball game. After hiking twenty-two miles with a forty pound pack due to the extra warm clothes I needed in the freeeezing weather, I decided to pass on that one. The next day I re-supplied, we found a laundromat and I got some clean clothes. That was a good thing as my hiking clothes smelled really bad. We ate hot food the next day at a place called The Lazy Hiker Brewing Company. We met a few other thru hikers who were eating there. They were all pretty much to themselves and did not appear to be very friendly but on our way out I introduced ourselves anyway. Little did I know that three of them would become a close part of my trail family. Jesse and Nate did not have trail names but would later be known as Flamingo and Frosting. Snow White was another member and I did not know her actual name until Pennsylvania. That night, Gail and I parked in the same place and the temperature got down to four degrees so I was elated that the van was at a balmy twenty-five degrees. Gail dropped me back off at the trailhead the next morning.

Dark Thirty: This is also known as hiker midnight and is anytime after the sun goes down and the thru hiker is tired. Sometimes it can be before the sun goes down but indicates you are going to hit the sack.

Nero: This is a day of hiking that is near zero and usually associated with a re-supply day. When you first start your hike, a nero may be one to five miles. At the middle of the hike, it can be anything less than double digits. Towards the end it could be less than fifteen miles.

My first nero was just about three miles and hiked in record time with the excitement of a warm bed (wooden platform indoors), hot shower, laundry for clean clothes, and lots of hot food. It started well before the sun had brightened the path on our way to Hot Springs, North Carolina, to stay at the Laughing Heart Hiker Hostel. The four in our hiker family put all of our clothes in the washing machine, and they came out only slightly less disgusting. Being the Good Samaritan, I did a little first aid for Balto's blisters and feet issues.

NNOTT: Nights Not on The Trail. This may mean that you stayed at a hostel, hotel, car, van, relative's, friend's house (some of whom you may have not met before), or other place to call it a night.

I came up with this because of the several nights that I slept in our van. The first was at Neel Gap when my tent and my body were soaking wet. It was great to spend the night sleeping on a mattress while my tent was hanging from one end of the vehicle to the other to dry a bit from being out in the rain for three days. It looked like a staged gypsy indoor encampment. It was almost heaven.

Hiker Hostel: This lodging caters to hikers and generally provides a platform to place your sleeping bag. Some of these offer laundry services, transportation to re-supply in a nearby town or to and from trailheads, or sale of food or hiker supplies. These hostels can vary from a converted garage to a shack to a three-star resort and everything in between. The ones I stayed in were usually pretty basic except for the Hostel of Maine which was three and a half hiker stars.

AYCER: All You Can Eat Restaurant. These can range from Asian cuisine to home style to pizza places. These were sought-after venues that would satiate the most voracious hunger.

Hiker Hunger: This is a feeling you get when, after being on the trail for a couple of months, your body has consumed all of the available body fat and needs more calories to keep you hiking. This is fully evident when after having eaten a large pizza, 6 bread sticks, a pint of chocolate fudge ice cream and a sixteen ounce Coke, you can't resist stopping on the way out of town for a half dozen donuts. And you are still hungry. This can actually be a dangerous health risk and you will need to pay attention to the number of calories you are using and the amount of food you are consuming.

Half Gallon Challenge: At the halfway point on the trail, there is a stop at Pine Grove Furnace State Park in Pennsylvania where you can buy and eat a half gallon of ice cream. The challenge is to eat it in less than an hour. If you do it you get a small wooden spoon inscribed with "Completed Half Gallon Challenge." It is a badge of courage I was able to complete.

Treecipitation: The rain that occurs when the wind blows water off the trees after the rain has stopped but it still feels like it is raining. You are still getting wet in the green tunnel.

ABCDEFGH (A thru H): Always Be Chewing, Drinking, or Eating For Great Hiking.

Alphabet(ABCDEFGHIJKLMNOPQRSTUVWXYZ by Starfish):Always Be Chewing, Drinking, or Eating For Great Hiking and Inspirational Journey to Katahdin. Let the Many Nice Opportunities and People Quickly Reveal Subtle Truths Upon the Voyage's Way and Xpress Your Zeal. This was the expanded version added by Starfish. She is a poetic wordsmith.

Thru Hiker: These hikers look a bit tattered, muddy, and fatigued. Their packs, clothing, and other equipment can look used but in good shape or totally destroyed towards the end of their journey. They, the hikers and equipment, smell like they have sweated heavily every day for a week or more and not bathed or showered because they haven't. Thru hiker and hiker trash can be used interchangeably towards the end of the hike.

Hiker trash: Hikers that have been on the trail for several weeks. They have turned the five second rule into the five minute rule into the five day rule into "It's only been laying on the trail for a few days and looks edible so yes, I would eat it." It is all relative. If it looks okay, it is probably edible. One of our trail family members found a sucker on the ledge of the privy and ate it. They will also eat the leftover food from your plate when eating in a restaurant. Sometimes they ask permission first and sometimes they will just wait until you leave the table. They also have a significantly low level of modesty.

Hiker legs: The strength in your legs that allows you to hike a twenty-five mile day with significant elevation change and still be able to stand up the next day without excruciating pain and do it again the next day and the next day and the next day....

Day hiker: On the other hand, a day hiker is someone who is out to hike on the trail for a day and then returns back home. They are usually identified by pristinely clean clothing, a fresh smile, and a fragrance of something fresh and great smelling. They don't smell like hiker trash which is described above.

Section Hiker: As mentioned before, this person does a section at a time, as time permits, in hope of eventually completing the entire trail. While this may seem more reasonable, it is in some ways, more difficult. This was pointed out by my friend Why Not. Section hikers hike a part of the trail for a week or two and then go back to their work or school. By the time they are starting to attain hiker legs, they are off the trail. They start this process all over again at the next attempted section.

Gear leprosy: When someone has incredibly bad luck with gear that rips, tears, breaks or malfunctions frequently and, usually, at the most inconvenient times of the hike. One of our trail family members had really bad gear leprosy.

PUDS: Pointless ups and downs. I first heard this term used at the Rice Field Shelter by a section hiker. Get over it. The ups and downs are the point. Otherwise, it is just walking. The elevation change from the beginning to the end of the trail is equivalent to summiting Mount Everest sixteen times. That is one of the reasons it is considered the most challenging of the long trails in the United States.

Vermud: Hiking in Vermont which is notorious for large sections of mass quantities of mud, even on the tops of ridges and mountains.

Rocksylvania: Hiking in Pennsylvania is notorious for long sections of sharp, protruding rock. Some are camouflaged by leaves and small twigs and attempt to damage your boots or shoes, and bruise and crush your feet.

The Whites: The White Mountains in New Hampshire are notorious for severe weather, especially ferocious winds, snow, sleet, hail, fog, clouds, and rain, and incredibly difficult climbs and descents any time of the year.

Ridge Runner: These are people that are paid or volunteer to be on the trail in certain sections like the national parks and some other areas for the hiking season. They assist hikers with issues and help enforce the rules at shelters and camping areas. They are a great source of valuable trail information and are generally very pleasant to work with. They are not law enforcement but can contact them for immediate response if need be.

Stealth Camp: Setting up your tent for the night in a location that is not a designated camping spot. Sometimes this is just a flat spot in the woods where no one has ever camped before and sometimes it is a spot that is well used and easy to identify. Some of my stealth sites were used by no one else before and, hopefully, because I adhered to the Leave No Trace rules, no one would detect that I had been there. I hiked past one of my stealth sites from the previous year and found there was no trace of my past visit for the night.

Trail Angel/Trail Magic: There is a whole chapter on Trail Angels and Trail Magic, and I have mentioned some of them in previous parts of this book. (See Chapter 6)

Trail Name: This is a name given to you while hiking on the trail or one you assume before you hike the trail and hope it will stick.

Ramen bomb: Ramen noodles prepared with mashed potatoes and occasionally other things like beef jerky or parmesan cheese or an assortment of dried vegetables or anything else you can think of to make your twelfth meal of Ramen palatable.

BPW (Base Pack Weight): This is the weight of your pack before you add food or water. I have found some hikers forget to add things like their phone, hiking poles, battery pack, video equipment, toilet tool, or other things they take but neglect to include so they can brag about the low BPW.

Trail Fam:A group of hikers that generally hike together or at least end at the same place at the end of the hiking day. (See Chapter 4)

Connecticut Challenge: This is the challenge of starting your hike in New York and ending in Massachusetts, passing through all of Connecticut, in one day. This is about fifty miles. It is not against the "rules" for the day to start at 12:01 AM and end at 11:59 the same day.

Several of the younger members of my trail family took this challenge. They stealth camped on the New York side of the road before you get into Connecticut. They got up at 2:30 AM to start their day's hike towards Massachusetts. They were met where the trail crossed a road near Kent, Connecticut, at about 7:00 AM for a Trial Magic breakfast provided by Cutie Angel. They arrived at the Sages in Massachusetts about 11:00 PM with a hiking day of 51 miles. Crazy kids.

Four State Challenge: Hiking straight through four states in one day. The day could start at 12:01 AM and end at 11:59 the same day. The best place to attempt this challenge starts in Virginia and passes through West Virginia and Maryland and ends in Pennsylvania. This is usually about 45 miles and requires stealth camping at the Virginia/ West Virginia state line and ends when you enter Pennsylvania when you get to Penn-Mar park.

Leave No Trace: This is a principle of leaving the least amount of impact on the environment you possibly can. Whatever you pack in, you pack out. Leave no evidence that you camped at a spot. There are whole books on the subject of how to have minimal impact on the wilderness environment while backpacking.

Sayings from the Trail

There are a few sayings that help prepare you for the trail ahead.

Remember on the Appalachian Trail what goes up continues to go up.

HIKE YOUR OWN HIKE.

Remember on the Appalachian Trail when you start to go down it doesn't mean that you are at the top and you may start upward again in a few feet.

An Appalachian Trail switchback switches from going straight up to going straight down.

Walk, eat, walk, eat, sleep, eat, walk, repeat.

It's cold. Keep walking. It's raining. Keep walking. It's hot. Keep walking. It's beautiful weather. Keep walking. Get the point? Keep walking, it is why we are here.

If you are hiking and the weather is really bad, just "Embrace the suck". (Attributed to Classic and Flamingo and a couple of others as well)

If you haven't seen a white blaze in a couple of miles you just may be in New Hampshire and you are not hiking on the AT.

If your GPS tracking on your phone sucks the life out of your battery, put it on airplane mode and low power mode. Also turn the data off on everything except the essentials as they suck the life out of your battery. This allowed me three days of batteries as opposed to one. (Thanks, Flamingo.)

If you travel past an Appalachian Trail Trailhead and your car suddenly swerves over to the parking area, you may just have the AT hiking addiction. There is no cure for this addiction.

You might be a thru hiker (Hiker Trash):

If you haven't showered in over a week.

If your wallet is really a zip lock bag.

If you have eaten three ramen meals in the same day but by adding Parmesan cheese, they became gourmet.

If you haven't driven a car in more than four months.

If your private bathroom is really just a pine tree.

If watering a tree means you need to pee.

If burying a cat means you are going to poop in the woods.

If the Wendy's bathroom is considered luxurious.

If bathing once a week is optional.

If you can wear one pair of your underwear five days or more.

(Front side, back side, commando, inside, outside. Repeat)

If that reddish dot on the trail is either a gummy or an Advil and you eat it anyway.

If your first aid kit is really just a small roll of duct tape.

If your food choices are based on the maximum amount of fat and calories per serving per gram.

If you have eaten off another person's plate in a restaurant and you've never met them before.

If you dream about consuming large quantities of food.

If you smell like really old chicken soup.

If you gag just a little when first climb into your sleeping bag.

These are just a few things that can differentiate between a regular hiker and a thru hiker

5

Trail Names and Trail Family

The third day of my hike, I met a very young couple. His trail name was Spruce Lee and her name was Shetalki. He was Asian American and his name was a take-off of Bruce Lee. She got her name because she talky a lot. We passed multiple times over the first two days of hiking. They were familiar faces and enjoyable to chat with. On the third day of hiking, it was raining and cold, and I came across Spruce and Shetalki sitting along the trail. He was trying to wrap his knee with an Ace bandage as he fell and twisted it. I offered to look at his knee and assessed that it was not too serious. I gave him a little friendly professional advice and asked if he needed any help to get to the trailhead. He said no and that just wrapping for him was helpful. I met them again the next day and he thanked me for the advice and said he was much better. He said "You are a Good Samaritan. Thanks." A couple of days later I offered to help a fellow hiker who I noticed had been limping by getting water for him from a water source accessed via a very challenging steep rocky trail. When I returned, he said, "Thank you. You are really a Good Samaritan." Thus, I received my trail name, the Good Samaritan. My trail family sparked some Biblical discussions about the

Good Samaritan, the Samaritan woman at the well, the significance of who Samaritans were, and what they were known for in Biblical times. Our discussions identified the cultural mores of that nation and, therefore, most of the time, they just called me Samaritan. I am not perfect by any stretch of the imagination. When we chat today, they just call me Samaritan. I accept that trail name with honor.

Trail names are a fun way to be identified on the trail without revealing your actual identity. You are allowed to be anonymous for an extended period of time or forever if you want. You can be your true self without any preconceived labels from your off-trail life. The people you meet will not know if you are a brain surgeon or lawyer or a ditch digger. It is a new start, so to speak. Some hikers assume a trail name before hitting the trail because they had a nickname or they picked one out to portray who they want to be or one they thought was just cool. If you allow the trail to give you a name, you run the risk that it may be based on a compromising moment. So, be sure you try not to do embarrassing things when you start out or you might get a name like Fartsack, Barf, Shitfoot, or Booger. Just sayin. You actually do not have to accept the trail name you are given but sometimes you do not have much of a choice.

Nathan hated the idea of a trail name but enjoyed classical music and classical literature. He was an attorney from Ohio. While sitting around the campfire at the Overmountain Shelter, several of my trail family, Starfish, Snow White, Flamingo, Frosting, and Physics racked their brains to come up with a trail name that Nathan would accept. He finally accepted the trail name Classic. It was classic, Classic.

A young lady from Alaska was part of our original trail family and received the trail name Balto. This was after the sled dog that inspired the running of the Iditarod. She was a feisty and energetic world traveler with a heavy pack and the name fit her well. She reported she was from Alaska where the men are men and the women win the Iditarod. She also said, "If you are not the lead dog, the scenery never changes." Sometimes that scenery is not all that bad to keep in view.

Jesse, who I met in Franklin, got his trail name from a Trail Angel who had an uncanny way of knowing hikers and gave several names that fit well. Flamingo was given his name after talking with him for only a few minutes. Later it was confirmed when Mission snagged a pink rubber duck from a video game at a pizza ACYER in Irwin, Tennessee.

Starfish, a young lady from Germany, was going to medical school in the United States in August. She wanted to become a physician to save the world. She told the story of the young person walking the beach after a violent storm had washed thousands and thousands of starfish onto the beach. One at a time, she began picking up the starfish and tossing them back into the ocean. A passerby derided and told her she would never be able to save them all. Her response was, "But I saved this one," as she threw it back and then picked another with the same response. Her kindness and compassion were evident in her personality and fit the story she told about her life mission and hence her trail name was Starfish. She would also write a poem about the day in each of the shelter's journals.

Nate was a young man from Florida who would purchase a container of frosting almost every time he re-supplied and eat the entire thing within a day or two and, therefore, he was given the name Frosting. He was encouraged to do so when someone else would purchase a two pound package of animal crackers. (The Good Samaritan would do that occasionally and share the treat as well.)

Physics was a junior in college going for a degree in physics. He was really smart and would write a mathematical equation in the shelter journal at each stop. Some of them were more than a whole page. He graduated the next year, and I am sure he landed a very good job analyzing data.

Dr. Thunder drank a cola drink called Dr. Thunder. I personally had not heard of that soda before but have seen it on shelves subsequently when I have been traveling.

Snow White had charcoal black hair and an extremely fair complexion. She was from Germany and started in mid February. The weather was pretty harsh, and she was about to call it quits by the end of the second week. She had hiked with a guy named Tie, and he told her to not quit on a bad day as that would mean the trail got the better of you. "Only quit on a good day after you have thought about it." Good advice, Tie.

We had a Legolas, Scamper, Tie, Indigo and a Comet as well. As this is a linear community, we did not always hike together or end the day at the same spot but generally we considered ourselves a Trail Family.

One hiker I met towards the end of my time on the trail told me he would come into camp and was asked many days in a row if he had a trail name yet. His reply would always be, "Nope." His trail name was Nope. We had an instant connection even though we had not ever hiked together before. I had heard of this hiker through trail journals and stories from other hikers who knew him.

I met another hiker whose name was Smalls. She was an experienced backpacker but tiny young lady who will be mentioned again when I talk a bit about gear.

One trail family that I knew and hiked with occasionally was the Blue Crew. The members were Farmer, Frozen, Catmando, Merica, and RD. Another eclectic group of avid hikers that will be friends for life. Farmer was retired from military special forces as a medic, student and soon to be hobby farmer, thus the trail name. Frozen is a hiking videographer that has a blog, frozenoutdooradventures. I am not sure how he got his trail name. Catmando is a retired landscape botanist that had retired after working for a large international hotel chain and worked for a national outdoor supply company. He had a wealth of knowledge and wisdom about the flora of the woods. I did not know Merica well. RD stands for "Resident Daddy" and was the youngest of that group. They all had two things in common, blue t-shirts and the love of hiking and the outdoors.

The trail promotes a linear community of hikers. We may meet someone one time or a few times and have seen their entries in one or more of the shelter log books. The trail gives us a bond from our shared hiking purpose. This community can also allow us to fit into a

Trail Family which is the group of hikers that have spent significant time together, usually at the end of the day and during town time. They may hike together for periods, share meals, and end their days at the same shelters or tenting spots. You may not see a person for several days or even a few weeks but pick up right where you left off and enjoy each other's company. This was true of the Frubble family to which I belonged. Frubble comes from the term "front bubble" as we were one of the largest groups to finish the trail early. It was strange when trail families' actual names were revealed. Although vastly different in age and probably ideologies, we still enjoyed each other's quirky personalities and were a close-knit family. Early in our family's journey after a day of hiking, we sat chatting while preparing to call it an evening. We delved into our backgrounds and experiences. I have a lot of those as I am an old guy. We would chat about our families, school, jobs, and friends, and of course, hiking. I would always ask, "Did you see the Bear?" They would exclaim "You saw a BEAR!" Most of the time I would say, "No, but I was wondering if any of you looked around enough to see a bear that might have been there". They laughed or at least groaned. A few times, I did see a bear that they had not. Later in the hike, I would replace bear with moose. I saw three moose on the journey, and two of them were close enough to throw a stick at. As a long time youth leader at my church and with Campus Life, I began asking youth group questions. I suggested that we should do "Hi/Low". What was your high and what was your low for the day? Most of our trail family were in their teens and twenties, and they thought that was a great idea. We did that every night we were together and a few times when I had cell coverage a group of our family would call and ask High/Low. Another evening around the campfire, I was asked about my children and some of the things we would do as a family. When I told them I would sing the "Good Night, Sweetheart" song to my kids at bedtime, they demanded I sing to them as well. Thus began an addition to our family traditions.

I would sing a lot on the trail, mostly to the birds, but occasionally when setting up for the evening. One time I was singing "Blue Moon" out loud to myself, and Frosting exclaimed that he had heard that song. I asked if it was on the radio, and he told me it was a video game he played. He asked if I would sing it to the group. I agreed. Two evening songs were added. Our evening traditions included a lot of chatting with Hi/Low and a couple of songs. At one rather small shelter in Virginia where our trail family was spending the evening, Starfish and Frosting set up their tents and we shared Hi/Low while preparing and eating food. I noticed that we were all in the sack except Starfish and Frosting who were sitting arms crossed at the picnic table, and it was getting chilly. I asked why they were not in their tents. They reported to me that I had not sung to everyone, so they just couldn't go to sleep without singing. The evening singing tradition was etched into our routine from that time on.

I sang many old hymns and my favorite worship song as I hiked every day. I also had a lot of time to talk to God and pray for my trail family, children, grandchildren and my wife.

Trail families come in all shapes and sizes and usually have not met before the trail. One good piece of advice that I got about trail families is that you should not be in one that does not fit your personality and hiking style. Hike your own hike. Don't try to hike faster or go slower than your pace. And don't fall in with an abusive or toxic personality group either. If you find yourself in such a group, take a zero or two and let that group hike past. Or if possible, put a few extra miles in to move on to avoid them and hang out with a group that fits your hiking style, pace, and personality. There is no sense in being stressed and miserable in the wilderness. Most all of the trail families I ran into supported each other and had great fun in good trail conditions and bad.

The trail is a linear community. There is an ebb and flow in the relationships but they are always there. Everyone who hikes the trail shares a special connection to others through the trail. You may read about events or people in the shelter journals or hear stories from other hikers about a person on the trail. When you happen to meet that person, the connection to that person is instant. It is like an old friend you have never met before. All are in the community, and some are family.

Snow White, Tie, Starfish, myself, Classic, Flamingo (front row), Frosting, and Legolas at the Graymour Spiritual Life Center.

The Frubble trail family. Flamingo, myself, Scamper, Classic, Physics, Dr. Thunder, Legolas, Starfish, and Comet at the Yellow Deli in Rutland Vermont. Evolution joined us for a day or so on the trail.

6

Approaching the Psychological Halfway Point

After leaving the Grayson Highlands, our trail family separated a bit as Classic was meeting his nephews and hiking with them in Shenandoah National Park. I had invited Flamingo to take a zero with me at my daughter's house for Easter. He needed to replace his shoes as they were duct taped together to stay on his feet. Gail would pick us up just before the Shenandoah National Park. Flamingo was about a half day behind me but I had assured him we would wait for him at the designated meeting place just before the entrance to Shenandoah National Park. That morning was April 19th, and it started out raining lightly. I had about eight miles to go before getting picked up. It was a nero. Within an hour, the weather went from raining off and on, to steady, to heavy, to a downright deluge. There was a literal river raging down the trail. My attempts to keep my feet dry were futile. By the time I got within two miles of the van, the trail was a river. At that point, the rain was warm as I walked through the water. I cleared the water run-off slots that were clogged with debris so the water would better drain from the trail. Sometimes the water would be up to my mid calves. I could take my time and enjoy the circumstances because I knew the van, dry clothing, and food was awaiting me as well as my lovely wife. We would have time before Flamingo arrived anyway. I was overjoyed when I spotted the white van, Tiny, in the parking area by the trail head. I was able to get out of my wet clothes and ate a family sized bag of potato chips and a Coke. About fifteen minutes later, we spotted Flamingo coming up the path with his walking stick he had named Wonder Boy. He took his pack off and placed it in the van, and then he hurled Wonder Boy off into the nearby bushes. When I told him we could take it with us, he said he would find another Wonder Boy when we got back on the trail. He dried off a bit and shed some of his wet clothes, and Gail drove us to civilization.

On our way to my daughter's house, I ate everything I could forage in Tiny. When we arrived, it was time for showers, laundry, and of course, food, lots of food.

On Saturday morning, it was sunny and warm, and Flamingo and I drove to the REI store in Rockville, Maryland to buy shoes and a few other supplies. I was not really sure if I was up for driving in traffic but we made it in one piece. We were in luck when we reached the store as it was the "Members Only REI Garage Sale", and I am a member. I found a puffy, a lightweight insulated jacket that would serve me well for the rest of my time on the trail and bought fuel for my Jet Boil. Flamingo found a pair of trail shoes so our mission was complete. That afternoon, we took a short hike with my grandson. Flamingo played the rest of the afternoon with Caleb and his toys. Saturday evening, we went to the Easter service at my daughter's church. The service and music were great, as usual. The sermon was about why we celebrate the death and resurrection of our Lord and Savior, Jesus Christ. After the service, we headed back for more food and a good night's sleep. Sunday there was a large breakfast to be enjoyed. Then the restlessness started creeping in with a strong desire to head back to the trail. Gail noticed and asked if we would like to head back to the trail today instead of tomorrow. We gathered our equipment and Gail took us back to the trailhead just outside the southern entrance to Shenandoah National Park in the middle of the afternoon. When we arrived, we donned our packs and got ready to hit the trail. Flamingo dashed off into the bushes and after just a few minutes he emerged holding his original Wonder Boy. We said goodbye to Gail and hiked on. As we entered the Park, we had to register, even though the road was closed. Gail would follow me through the park but could not use this entrance because the road was closed due to recent high winds and severe weather that knocked down a large number of trees over thirty miles of the road at the southern entrance. Cell coverage was irregular, so communication and coordinating our meeting places was difficult at best. It was also complicated by my inability to know how far I would hike on any given day. The Park is an excellent place for you to achieve long miles as the trail is more gradual and well maintained. We were able to meet up at a couple of campgrounds in the park where the trail went alongside the campground. I knew I was in the right spot when I spied two small oranges atop of a trail marker and a red hiking pole leaned against it; both were from my Trail Angel, Cutie. The first campground had a coin operated shower and camp store. A hot shower and ice cream were real treats. Our fellow campers were very friendly and quiet. The next spot was stealth at a trailhead. The trail passed right along the third campground, so I was able to spot Tiny with Gail sitting in a chair next to it. It was a quiet spot but not so friendly. The next night was a trailhead stealth spot. That allowed me to have four NNOTTs before Gail traveled back to my daughter's home for a few days.

West Virginia has the fewest miles on the trail but Harpers Ferry is the physiological hallway point of the trail as it is the town where the Appalachian Trail Conservancy is and is the midpoint check in. When you get there, you feel a sense of accomplishment because you have passed the 1,000 mile mark and hiked through the "Roller Coaster". This is a thirteen-mile section that has some of steeper climbs and descents so far on the trail. I was particularly elated on this hiking day as I passed the 1,000-mile mark, did most of the Roller Coaster and did a thirty-one-and-a-half-mile day. The day got better when I met four young ladies that were having a girl's hike reunion and they gave me a beer I could have with my dinner. I could have more beer if I stayed at the shelter with them. I chose hiking over beer. To top it all off, when I set up my stealth campsite, I had cell service and a call from one of my daughters. In two days, I would be in Harpers Ferry and on a Nero and have a NNOTT. Also, there would be a hot shower, laundry, clean clothes, re-supply, lots of food, and of course, my wife and family.

My daughter, wife and grandson, Caleb, joyfully met me at the Appalachian Trail Conservancy. While there, Caleb wanted to hike the trail, so he and I headed out towards the trail and hiked through some of the historic areas of Harpers Ferry. We crossed the railroad bridge over the Potomac River that took us from West Virginia into Maryland and then back to be picked up by my wife and daughter. I would spend a NNOTT at my daughter's. The next day, I was dropped off at the bridge and hiked north. Gail headed back home to Indiana. It was Flip Flop Days in Harpers Ferry and I knew as I traveled, the trail would be rather crowded. Sure enough, there must have been forty tents set up in the camping area around Dahlgren Backpack Campground as I passed by. I planned to put in big miles for the next few days to miss some of the congestion caused by the Flip Floppers going north. My trail legs did not fail me, and after three days, I left almost all of the flip floppers behind me. Passing through Pine Grove Furnace State Park, I was able to use a flush toilet and refill my water bottles but was denied taking the Half Gallon Challenge as that park of the park was not yet open. I would come back for that after my hike was completed.

I traveled several days alone again, especially after I knew I was a day behind my trail family. I was aware of where they were because I read entries in the shelter logs. Detailed physics equations, poems by Starfish, and the picture of a flamingo were tell-tale signs my family was just ahead.

7

Hiker Hunger

Hiker hunger is a phenomenon that develops in most thru hikers when they are depleting their body fat stores and have an almost insatiable appetite. The average hiker will cover fifteen to twenty-five miles a day wearing a twenty-five to forty pound pack and climb up and down 500 to 3000 feet of elevation change. The calorie consumption will vary between 4,000 and 8,000 calories each day. What do you have to eat in a day that will provide you with that many calories? Is it even possible to consume that much? Do the math. You will use a lot of calories to provide the energy requirement for that type of work out day after day. Calories are king, and your body really can't get enough of them. I used an average of about 6,000 calories per day while hiking and suffered from a bit of malnutrition during the last four to six weeks of my hike. I had no fat pads on my hips or feet or anywhere for that matter. My hair became dry and brittle. I lost hair on my chest and my finger, and toenails became brittle. It was not a fun side effect of the decreased nutrition. It really gives credence to the moniker, ABCDE-FGH. Always Be Chewing, Drinking, and Eating For Great Hiking.

That evening after hiking a thirty-one mile day through the Roller Coaster (lots of elevation change) in Virginia, I passed the 1,000 mile mark on the trail. I was stealth camping the end of the "Roller Coaster" in Virginia and had just set up my tent and was eating my dinner. I was surprised and pleased that I had phone signal and that my daughter called me on a particularly strenuous hiking day. The conversation went something this, "Hey, Dad, how are you doing? I just got pinged from your hike tracker and I'm amazed that you did a thirty-one today. You are amazing! What did you eat today?" I thought that to be a little strange but reported the food I consumed. I went through a list of everything I could think of that I had consumed that day, including the beer I was given by 4 ladies. "Wow, Dad! That is great!", she responded. "And do you know how many calories was that?" I quickly added up a rough estimate which came to about 4,800 calories. She then asked, "So, where did you get the other 2,400 calories you burned because your tracker said you used a total of 7,200 calories today?" I had forgotten that when she gets a ping at the end of my hiking day, it has all the technical details of my hiking including time, distance, pace, elevation change, and estimated calories expended. I was not able to answer that question very well. She then let me know that I probably needed to keep track of my calorie usage a bit better. She texted me a list of highest calorie per gram foods that I could get on my food resupply days. Parmesan cheese has the highest calories per gram of any cheese and keeps well without refrigeration. It also makes Ramen more palatable. Macadamia nuts are also high calorie per gram sources of fuel.

With this in mind, if you are using a couple thousand more calories than you take in, you will lose weight quickly and hiker hunger will develop due to this caloric deficit, not to mention possible malnutrition. Hikers search out AYCERs, All You Can Eat Restaurants. We can consume a large pizza, two large bowls of pudding, three pop tarts, a salad, and drink a twenty-four ounce soft drink before contemplating what we will have for dessert. I did this several times on the journey. We will sport a nice little food baby while we are looking for dessert. This hiker hunger can last for several months after leaving the trail as well, and sometimes hikers rebound to a higher weight than their pre-hike weight. That has not been the case for me. I lost twenty-five pounds and have only gained about eighteen back.

Pine Grove Furnace State Park is the technical halfway point of the Trail and at their concession, they challenge thru hikers to eat a half gallon of ice cream in an hour to win a little wooden spoon that has "I completed the Half Gallon Challenge" imprinted on it. It was not yet open when I traveled through, and I was horribly disappointed but vowed to return after completion of my hike.

At the end of my journey, my wife and I decided to go to Weymouth, Massachusetts, to visit Why Not, with whom I hiked the last four weeks and made the final intense climb to the summit of Katahdin. We visited for a day and the next day decided to take the ferry over to Boston to hike the historic Freedom Trail. While I really like visiting historical sights, I had extreme difficulty paying attention to the great history as I was distracted by the plethora of Dunkin Doughnuts shops around every corner and a great variety of sumptuous eateries along the way. I did limit myself to a half dozen glazed donuts and a visit to an Italian grocery for items to make sandwiches.

8

Trail Magic and Trail Angels

Trail Magic is something that happens unexpectedly on the trail that brightens your day or helps your hike in some way. It can be an encouraging word, a ride into town for re-supply, a warm place to sleep, or a full seven course meal. I mentioned a few Trail Magic events previously that happened for me and that I provided while section hiking. There are quite a few people that visit the trail who are not hikers that specifically provide treats and other food to hikers.

During my second week on the trail, I was moving a bit faster than most of the other hikers so I had not fallen into a trail family at that point. I planned to eat dinner a little early at a small wayside where the trail crossed a road and then hike several more miles before making camp. I crossed the road and saw a couple of picnic tables in the distance just past a little bridge over a small creek. I was delighted to know I could take off my pack for a few minutes and prepare my early dinner of chicken and rice and a pop tart on an actual picnic table. I was also glad to be able to filter some cold water from the stream. As I approached the bridge, I noticed that someone had dumped trash in the creek, and I was really disappointed and a bit mad. As I drew closer, I noticed that the pop cans appeared to be unopened. My irritation quickly turned into a huge smile. My spirits were immediately lifted when I realized this was TRAIL MAGIC! I don't know who was responsible for this little extravagance, but it sure lifted my mental state having an ice-cold Coke to drink with my dinner.

When hiking through the Smoky Mountains, we came to the parking lot at Newfound Gap and there was a minivan with a gentleman standing at the back with the hatch up revealing bins of food. There was bread and cold cuts, fruit, doughnuts, HoHos, Twinkies, a large variety of chips and candy bars, pop, and water. The gentleman said that alcohol was not allowed in the park but the ranger gave him a case of beer that was confiscated from some youth, and he passed those out on a limited basis, too.

Hiking in Grayson Highlands, I was on top of a grassy and treeless part of the state park just after Buzzard Rock. It had rained most of the night before and the trail was narrow, rutted, muddy, and very slippery. It was mostly sunny this particular late morning but the temperatures in the mid-forties and it was breezy. There were patches of snow still lingering on the ground. We were not enjoying this particular day of hiking due to the cold and trail conditions. I could see Classic about a quarter mile in front of me, head down and marching straight on without distraction. It appeared that his mission was just to get through this day as quickly as possible. Occasionally, he would pass a day hiker or two, and Classic tended to share very few pleasantries and kept on hiking. I, on the other hand, generally asked the fellow hikers about their hike or where they were going for the day and if they were thru hiking, section hiking, or day hiking. It gave me an excuse for a few seconds to rest.

I noticed as we were trudging down a particularly muddy section, Classic actually stopped for a few seconds seemingly to exchange pleasantries and then moved on down the trail. That was strange to me as that was a bit out of character for Nathan to stop to speak with a day hiker along the way. As I hiked on and got closer, I noticed the hiker Classic had stopped to chat with was a slender rather attractive young lady approaching wearing running shorts and hosting a day pack. I thought to myself that the reason he had stopped was just that she was very attractive. As we approached, she immediately stepped off the trail. This was a good indication that she was a veteran hiker familiar with hiking etiquette, despite it being obvious by her pack and fresh clean clothes that she was a day hiker. I stopped and asked my usual conversational questions to find out she had thru hiked in 2016. She then placed her hiking poles in one hand and reached her other hand towards the back of her pack producing a bite sized Snickers bar. This small sweet treat was not much in the way of calories but boosted my spirits tremendously and lightened my step. Trail Magic!

Trail Angels come in all shapes and sizes and can be as random as those chance meetings on the trail. Some I met and some were totally anonymous. They can be a cooler left at a trailhead with a note for thru hikers to enjoy to someone helping you in a time where the trail has not been very nice to you or you have miscalculated re-supply. Some have stories I can share with you and others I cannot.

One Trail Angel, known as Cutie Angel, would wait at trail heads while waiting for her husband to meet her and hand out Clementine oranges. She would take their trash and give them an encouraging word while she waited for me. I would be the recipient of a night in our van, fresh clothing, and lots of food. I have the best wife and she is a Trail Angel. On several occasions, she traveled from Indiana with homemade Italian beef, potato salad, coleslaw, fruit, candy, and delectable chocolate chip cookies. She was very appreciated by many hikers and especially my trail family.

When we approached Glenwood, New Jersey, we traveled close to Tie's home. I got a text to see if I would like to be picked up and spend the night there. It meant a hot shower, laundry, home cooked food, and sleeping indoors. I had hiked alone most of the day, my feet were wet, and it was cold. Debbie is a great cook. How could I resist? Debbie picked me up at Lovemma Road after gathering Snow White, Frosting, Starfish, and Classic. It was at least an hour drive back to their house, but it was well worth it and much appreciated. The next morning, Debbie dropped me off where I was picked up, and I headed north. She would pick us up again the next afternoon at Lakes Road for another NNOTT. Debbie would pick the others in our group up again another night, but I was comfortable back on the trail as I hike quite a bit slower, and they would have had to wait for me. This is Trail Magic that is above and beyond. Thanks, Debbie and Tie.

Tie, Gail, Classic, and Dr Thunder after being fed by Gail, Cutie Angel.

Gail feeding breakfast to our trial family that were taking the Connecticut Challenge.

On one occasion of feeding thru hikers in Connecticut, Gail had set up on an out of the way road where the trail crossed waiting for me and the rest of the trail family. I was a little early that day and was going to have a NNOTT. As I helped get the food out, I noticed a small black car coming down the road towards us and it slowed way down as it passed and did not accelerate until almost out of sight. I thought it to be a little strange but had things to help Gail with to get set up for the hungry hikers. We fed the entire trail family and the Honeymoon Hikers as they stopped by. As darkness started to settle and the last hikers left to spend the night at the shelter about two miles up the trail, I was helping clean up and stow items in Tiny. We talked about finding a flatter place to park that was safe, but Gail said this road had no remotely flat parking as she traveled it a couple of times looking for night parking. As we were packing, I noticed that same small black car traveling very slowly towards us and then past. It pulled off the road about thirty yards in front of us and backed up right in front of our van. "Uh Oh!" I thought, "we may be in trouble." A man got out and walked back and said hello. He asked if we were doing Trail Magic. We told him we were and that I was thru hiking. He was a section hiker and attended paramedic training earlier that day and was headed back home. He missed hiking and thought he would stop and chat a little if we were still there on his return. Before he left, I asked if there were any safe and flat places to park close by. He said there were no places on this road but he only lived ten minutes away, and we could park in his driveway. We could also have a hot shower, sleep inside, and have hot coffee and breakfast as well. It was just he and his wife and two dogs at home. They were up at five o'clock every morning. We followed him to his house. His driveway was flat, and he had two huge, very friendly lap dogs. We enjoyed their company and the dogs and chatted for several hours after we took a shower. His wife was a teacher and had to work the next morning. We thanked them for their wonderful hospitality and bid them good night before retiring for the night in Tiny. John was out tapping on the window at 5:15 AM to let us know that coffee was ready and waiting and that Joan was almost ready for school. We were truly blessed by their generosity.

The Leap Frog Café is one of the full time Trail Magic providers, run by Fresh Ground, that travels along the trail supporting hikers in any way he can. He drives an older but well-maintained van and sets up at trailheads to feed hungry thru hikers. He will feed you if you are a section hiker or even a day hiker. His main focus is for thru hikers, either SOBO or NOBO. He has a really slick setup. A large canopy covering a washing station, propane cookers, multiple snack bins, chairs, and a few tables. He takes great pride in his gourmet hiker meals. He has famous banana and chocolate chip pancakes and makes a mean omelet. At the end of the day, he will even transport hikers to town for re-supply. I got to know Fresh Ground while on my thru hike and was the recipient of many surprise meals. Fresh Ground works in the winter as an electrician and spends the spring, summer and fall hiking season taking care of hikers. He does take donations to help him support his trail magic efforts but donations are not required or even asked for on the trail. He now is a 503C charitable organization. He posts regularly on Facebook and Instagram, and you can find him there regularly. He is a true Trail Angel.

Trail magic can take many forms. Sometimes it is a little snack or a full meal. It can be a ride into town or a tip on a town's free amenities. It can be letting you camp in someone's yard or even take a shower at someone's home. It can be as simple as an encouraging word from a fellow hiker. It is something unexpected and special in the hiking world and we truly appreciate it whenever it happens.

9

After the Midpoint

I hiked my way north, said goodbye to Maryland and entered Pennsylvania. It is known for its rocky path, hence the nickname Rocksylvania. It did not disappoint in this regard. The rocks were sharp and sometimes disguised by leaves or other unassuming debris on the trail. When you thought you were stepping on leaves, a sharp little dagger of a rock would jump up and punish the bottom of your foot. Repeat this thousands of times and you can develop issues with your feet in Rocksylvania. I am pretty sure that is where most of the numbness in both of my feet started. As I hiked toward Pine Grove Furnace State Park, I was anticipating trying the Half Gallon Challenge only to find it was mid-week and would be closed on weekdays until Memorial Day. I was terribly disappointed but at least fresh water and flush toilets were available.

My daughter would take me off the trail at Duncannon on May 5th. I would have another zero to resupply, and I would pick up a new pair of OBOZ hiking boots. I would also eat lots of food, wash clothes, shower and sleep in a warm bed and enjoy the company of my daughter, son-in-law, and my wonderful grandson and his ever-inquisitive mind. No less than a barrage of one million questions were asked of me. I loved it. During this time their family was diligently working on adopting a little girl from Ukraine. Tetiana would officially join their family later in the year. I enjoyed hearing all of the details that were going into the process of helping her become a part of our family. She was already in our hearts and loved her dearly. She has become an avid little hiker.

On the way back to the trailhead, we would meet up for breakfast with some friends who moved to Pennsylvania many years before. It was great to catch up with Kurt and Tina. I headed north on a full stomach and with new boots. My trail family was still a day ahead.

I hiked alone most of the time but occasionally passed a section hiker who would pass me when I stopped to take a lunch break. He was out for five days, and this would be his last night on the trail. He would have one more day and then had to return to work. After my night's stop, I would have only one more day before reaching Delaware Water Gap and heading into New Jersey. It had rained off and on all day, but cleared up just before arriving at the Leroy Smith Shelter. When I got to the shelter, there were section hikers there. A young couple and another young man with two large dogs and their wet gear was sprawled everywhere around the shelter. They were attempting to light a fire in the soggy woodland. The wood was wet but, never fear, I had my trusty micro-bellows. The fire started to engage quite nicely after only a few minutes of work. I set up my space in the shelter and cooked dinner. While I was cleaning up, the section hiker arrived, and I said, "We meet again." He prepared his dinner and as he was finishing and enjoying the fire, he said, "Wouldn't this be a perfect fire for s'mores?" We all agreed with mildly long faces. Then, with a larger-than-life grin, he produced chocolate bars, marshmallows, and graham crackers. All of us enjoyed the tasty treat and thanked him profusely. Another great example of Trail Magic.

Trail Magic, s'mores.

I stayed at the Methodist Church Hiker Hostel in Delaware Water Gap the next night and met the NOBO Bros. The ability to re-supply was poor and expensive, and the food choices were minimal. The ice cream shop a block down from the church was fantastic, though. The best re-supply required a twenty mile trip to another town to shop at WalMart which I did not have the energy to do. As usual, I started early the next morning, and the rain was steady and cold. I hiked out of the Gap and into New Jersey hoping to do a twenty-six-mile day. I was wearing my rain slicker, but I quickly realized my hiking pants were getting totally soaked. My upper body was also soaked from profuse sweating. After only a few miles I started to feel cold. When you are cold, I am sure you only need to hike a little faster to warm up. As a point of information, increased energy usage cannot make you warm when you are already wet and cold. After about eight miles, I was feeling very cold and starting to shiver, the first signs of hypothermia. At 10.6 miles, I came to a gravel road that had a small sign that read "MOC .5 Left", the Mohican Outdoor Center. I absolutely hate traveling off the trail more than two-tenths of a mile for any reason other than a Nero, Zero or re-supply. Another way to warm up is to eat something. I tried to get a granola bar from the front pouch on my pack. I could not get a grip on the zipper to open the pouch. I had to take off my pack and use two hands to open it. I struggled to retrieve the granola bar and then used my teeth and hands to force the package open. I had lost all manual dexterity and strength in my hands. I then had a short conversation with myself.

> "Hey you only have sixteen miles to go to get to the shelter. Then you can get out of the wet clothes and warm up in the shelter in your sleeping bag. Can I do that without being able to eat anything because I can't feel my fingers and my hands don't work? I could hike faster. How has that been working? Hmmm, not so well. I hate having to walk an extra mile off the trail. That is a half mile there and a half mile back. What would your wife think when they find your body, and they have to tell her, 'Your husband died of hypothermia because he was stupid.'?" Argh.

I made a wise decision. At the Center, the staff were very helpful and understanding. I was able to dry out some of my gear and myself and had a massive second breakfast. I helped get the fire in the fireplace going and that helped me and a few others warm up as well. After drying out a little, eating a lot, and drinking a pot of coffee, I warmed up enough to get back on the trail and made a twenty-six mile day to end up at Brink Shelter.

Some of my trail family had friends meet them on the trail to hike with them. Usually, friends do not have hiker legs and you slow down significantly. Classic increased his mileage significantly to allow him to hike with his nephews and stay in sync with the trail family. I hiked with Jacob, my oldest grandson, but it was needed relief for me. Comet and Snow White also hiked with friends for a few days, as well. Snow White had dropped behind a bunch of miles and bypassed some of the trail to catch the trail family while Comet's friend, Tofu Jerky, was able to keep up.

I again traveled alone much of the time after having a couple of nights at Tie and Debbie's house. The hiking was relatively flat as I headed towards the Fingerboard Shelter. I had just resupplied so my pack was heavy. I stored my food in a bear canister that was recommended by the Appalachian Trail Conservancy. I fit everything in the canister except a couple of bags of beef jerky and a couple of bags of dried apples. I did not see another hiker use a bear canister the entire time I hiked on the AT. This is probably because it is heavy, three-and-a-half pounds, and is difficult to stow in your pack. I was wondering what I would do with the two bags of beef jerky and two bags of dried apples that Gail had made and sent in my recent mail drop. I thought I would take the chance and keep them in my sleeping bag. To heck with the bears and those ferocious mice.

When I approached the Fingerboard, there were two section hikers already in the shelter. After the usual introductions, they asked if I was going to hang a bear bag. I told them I had a bear canister that would hold everything except jerky and apples. It was recommended that food be stored in the shelter as there were bears that were able to retrieve from the hangs. I knew I could eat a lot but still was unable to make room for all of my food. After eating, I packed the canister to the maximum and placed it on a flat stoop about 100 feet from the shelter. As I was contemplating my sleeping arrangements, Flamingo arrived and started setting up his tent just behind the shelter, and it was dark thirty. A few minutes later, Legolas arrived and I told him about the bear activity and my food storage dilemma. I had never before slept with my food as I don't like the idea of mice chewing through my stuff for dinner. He told me bears could not get his hang, and I was welcome to throw extra food into his bag. He was resupplying in two days and was pretty empty. That would be great, and I hit the sack. I could hear him cooking and then it became quiet, and he did not sleep in the shelter even though there was one spot left on the platform.

About 9:30 or so, I heard clanking of cookware and thought Legolas must have decided to gather his bear bag to move on, and it must have been stuck. Then I heard scratching on the tree that sounded like a gigantic squirrel was scampering up and down. As I came to my senses, I realized that it really was probably a bear climbing the tree and had gotten hold of the bear bag cord. I got my head lamp and pointed it in the direction of the noise and could make out a large black shape going up the tree. It was a bear!

The bear would climb up the tree and out on the branch where the bag was tethered and bounce. Then it would climb down and grab the cord and pull a few times. Thus, the clanking of the cookware inside.

Up the tree, out on the branch, down the tree, pull the cord. It repeated this process for forty-five minutes while the occupants of the shelter watched with amazement with our headlamps illuminating the process. The bag came crashing down and there was no more clanking. We saw in the distance two sets of fluorescent eyes staring in the direction of the shelter.

I looked for my canister which had been knocked over and rolled about ten feet down the hill but was unscathed. We briefly looked for the bear bag, but there was no trace. Evidently the bear was satisfied with the jerky and apples and the meager portions of Legolas's supplies. The greatest loss was the stove and cooking utensils. We all headed back to the shelter to call it a night after the excitement.

As I drifted off to sleep, I heard a loud scream from the hiker beside me, "Hey! There's a bear!" Sure enough, at the edge of the shelter about five feet from our heads loomed a large black shape. It did not run away but slowly turned and slowly lumbered toward the back of the shelter. As we yelled for him to get out of there, I imagined him to be saying, "Who me? You mean I can't come in and have another snack? Oh, okay. I will just see if there are any morsels out back behind the shelter." That was where Flamingo and Legolas had set up their tents. We watched the bear cruise within inches of each of the tents as he circled back around the shelter. We watched the bear lumber around behind the shelter and then down the hill in front of us. For quite some time we saw two pairs of eyes in the distance until they vanished. Flamingo spent the rest of the night sleeping in the shelter with his food. Legolas stayed in his tent.

Flamingo was up about twenty minutes after I was in the morning. I left some packets of instant oatmeal and chicken Ramen for Legolas as the bear had all his food. I had forgotten he was vegetarian and got my food back a few days later. I had heard the Shaker Campsite farther up the trail had bear issues as well, so I planned my hiking and camping to avoid that spot. One crazy bear encounter was enough for me. Within a couple of days our trail family was back together again. I planned to get to the Graymoor Spiritual Life Center and would meet most of our trail family there again. It's a good place to stay for thru hikers. It was great to have the whole group together in one place with plenty of shelter room. Those present were Classic, Starfish, Physics, Snow White, Frosting, Flamingo, Tie, and Legolas.

The next day, May 18th, the usual members started early, and I stopped for a second breakfast with Classic, Tie, and Snow White. Snow White is always cheerful, and this day was no different. However, when she said "I am glad we all stopped together, and I want to tell everyone that I am leaving trail when we get to Pawling, New York, this afternoon. I will take the train to New York City and then fly to visit my friend in Florida. Those are things I want to do before I catch a flight back to Germany. It is a beautiful sunny day. Tie told me when we were still in North Carolina that you can't quit on a bad day. I will never be able to make up for the miles I lost on the trail, and I am very tired." Starfish and Physics joined us a bit later and we were all saddened by the decision but we all respected her wishes. We all hitchhiked into Pawling, New York, and purchased pastries at the local bakery as a going-away treat. We said our goodbyes at the bakery near where she would catch the train. Walking back toward the trail, we stopped for a few supplies before thumbing a ride back to the trailhead. It was a subdued time of hiking, and we all were thinking how much courage it took to make that decision to end her hike and that we would miss Snow White's company on our journey.

We hiked north for a few days and were planning a Zero at the Yellow Deli in Rutland, Vermont. They had a work-for-stay or a donation-for-stay. I chose to work and was able to help prep a floor in an upstairs meeting room for flooring. I worked for a couple of hours and was able to chat with some of the church members that were a part of the Twelve Tribes of Israel. They live communally and share everything and own nothing. They invited all of the hikers to a free meal and celebration at their local community center that Friday evening. Several of us attended the meal and celebration. The food was fish and lots of cooked vegetables. The celebration was a lot of dancing. Some of the Frubble participated but I did not dance. They also invited anyone who may want to see their farm to come on the next day. I chose to do my re-supply, repair some of my equipment. eat, and rest up a bit. I had a water bottle holder on my pack that needed some Velcro replaced. I went up the block to a wedding dress shop to see if I could purchase some Velcro. The shop owner did not have any for sale but gave me enough to do the repair and wished me good luck on my journey.

In the process of wandering around Rutland looking for a restaurant, I met a gentleman who directed me to a place to eat and joined me. In the conversation at dinner, we chatted about a lot of things hiking and also about my remodeling of our van into a mini motor home. He also was converting a bus into a motor home and took me to a warehouse to showed me the gutted city bus he had purchased. We discussed his plans to make it his home. He took me back to the Deli and wished me luck in my travels. I organized my pack with new supplies and headed to the community room where someone had brought day old pastries and a half pan of brownies. I ate most of the brownies and a few of the pastries. I met a hiker from Boston completing his journey for a hike he started in 2017. He injured his knee and took several months to rehab. His trail name was Why Not. In our conversation, he reported he would be taking a couple of Zeros in three or four days in Woodstock, New Hampshire, to meet his wife and some friends. Several of our trail family were planning to take the early bus back to the trailhead to continue our journey north the next day, so I said goodnight and headed for my bunk. I planned to take the bus back to the trailhead with the trail family.

Why Not and I would pass each other frequently along the trail over the next several days. He left the trail at Woodstock, and I headed north to Lincoln, New Hampshire, where I would meet my grandson, Jacob.

On June 4th, we ended in a shelter at Moose Mountain. Upon arriving at the shelter, Dr. Thunder had gathered firewood and was working on starting a fire. As that is one of my favorite things to do, I got my micro-bellows out and assisted in getting the fire going. After the fire was blazing, Dr. Thunder pulled out fixins for s'mores he had purchased at the last re-supply. Our entire trail family was happy with the treat. To our surprise and delight, who comes walking into camp but Snow White? She had flown back from Germany and into Rutland to complete the hike with the trail family. She brought German chocolates for all of us to share. We were all elated to see her. Our trail family was back together again on the trail. We had s'mores and fancy German chocolates and good conversations. Life was good.

10

Equipment and Stuff

There is always a dilemma for backpackers. We must balance weight and size versus comfort and cost. The really lightweight and effective gear is very expensive. There are some homemade items that are very inexpensive and lightweight but may not be reliable. Here is where product reviews and different hiking blogs can be very helpful in making those equipment decisions. Some websites I have visited are **Frozen Outdoor Adventures** and **Homemadegear.com**. (Frozen was a thru hiker I traveled with occasionally and he was part of the Blue Crew trail family.) I also subscribed to CARIN product review for several years before my adventure and found some very useful light-weight items. With Carin you pay a monthly or annual fee and they send you $30 to $50 dollars' worth of products to try. It can be food, clothing, equipment, mapping services, or a variety of other items. I still take many of those items on every adventure.

After about 700 miles on my first pair of Oboz Bridgers mid-height hiking boots, I thought I would wear my running shoes for a week while my replacement boots came in. That was a mistake. In one day, I developed two blisters on each foot and after the second day there were a total of seven blisters, and they were painful. Four on one foot and three on the other, plus I was missing two additional toe nails. I went back to wearing my old hiking boots but still had painful feet due to the blisters. Snow White noticed my misery and recommended puncturing the blister with a needle and thread, leaving the thread in to allow it drain and to heal faster. I didn't have a needle or thread but one of my friends, Tie, gave me his sewing kit for the procedure. It was difficult to pierce the callous but I got it accomplished on the foot with the four blisters and let the thread stick out about half an inch. If you do not have thread, you could use dental floss. As a controlled experiment, on the other foot, I just drained the blisters. The next day, there was no pain in the threaded foot but the punctured blisters without the thread were painful for two weeks. The thread allowed for the serous fluid of a blister to drain out and reduced the fluid pressure that tears the skin further and enlarges the blister. It lets the skin recover more quickly. At the same time, Tie was nursing a knee injury so we slowed down and hiked together for several days. That was the first night I have ever slept at a gas station, Quick Mart, Deli. (Never did that before.) New experiences abound

Not only is it important to know what gear you need, but it's equally vital to know the best way to get the most from your stuff. On one occasion in New Jersey when I was hiking by myself, I knew that within a few miles I would cross a road and be close to a place where I could do a little re-supply and get some hot deli food. Classic and the Honeymoon Hikers tipped me off to this place on the trail. I spent a good portion of my morning daydreaming about the possibility of ice cream, doughnuts, or other tasty treats. As I hiked, I noticed two young ladies hiking towards me with backpacks. They each sported a large gourmet looking coffee cup in one hand as they approached. The second young lady did not have a trail name but the first young lady's trail name was Smalls. This was for an obvious reason as she commented that she was not only short but proportionally small as well. She was wearing a midriff t-shirt that revealed her belly button ring and low-rise hiker pants showing her hip bones. The hip belt of her pack was resting snuggly on her skin over those hip bones. I couldn't help but stare as I had been battling blisters and sores on my iliac crests (hip bones) due to the loss of any fat pads in my body and the friction from my heavy pack's hip belt rubbing off the skin. I told her I would mention her in my book. From that day on, I would roll up my t-shirt and roll down my hiking pants before donning my pack and cinching up the hip belt. The bleeding stopped after a few days and wounds healed in a couple of weeks. The bruises were still present for several months after completing the hike. The fat pads are still pending. Thanks, Smalls.

The most accurate weather at the shelters along the trail is **ATweather.org** and if you get signal, it is very helpful in preparing for your day or more importantly, your night. Verizon seemed to have the best cell coverage in the trail almost 90% of the time, usually at the top of a mountain or at least while traveling along a ridge.

There are many options for cooking on the trail. One hiker I met had a trail name of Cold Soak and that is one way not to cook on the trail. It is efficient but takes planning and every meal is, well, cold. You place your food in a bag with water as you hike all day and it is usually edible by the time you stop for dinner. The **MSR** is a very lightweight cooking device but usually uses more fuel and gets fourteen to sixteen burns from an eight ounce canister. I had a Jet Boil so I decided not to cook in a pan but mostly use it for meals where you just add boiling water. I would get twenty-four to twenty-eight burns per eight ounce canister. The Jet Boil is very efficient. It is always good to have a back-up lighter as my igniter broke three-quarters of the way through my hike.

Collapsible bowl. I purchased a cheap collapsible heat tolerant bowl that I would put freeze-dried meals in and just add boiling water. After eating, I would run the bowl through the dishwasher (lick it clean), and it was ready for the next meal. When it was cold, I would also have hot chocolate before hitting the sack. Again, I would also run it through the dishwasher. It helps to keep things clean, and you get all of the calories possible. I would skip the water boiling process when it got warmer and just eat four or five heaping spoonfuls of the mix as dessert. It would give me 400 to 500 extra calories. Some of my hiking friends would actually cook meals meaning their pots had to be washed with soap and water. They would accumulate leftovers on a regular basis to avoid the grunge build up.

Carbon fiber trekking poles worked best for me. Poles tend to give you a better way to balance and keep your hands from swelling when they hang at your side. The carbon fiber ones are significantly lighter and pretty durable. Check the availability of replacement parts, and the warranty as they are not quite as durable as aluminum poles. One of my pole tips broke in Vermont, and they did not have replacement parts available. They would not honor the warranty as I ordered from a third party, and they were a discontinued model. A ski shop in Lincoln found replacements for the lower sections for $19.00 that worked beautifully. I still use them today.

Electronics and battery systems. I used my cell phone and had insurance on it before starting the hike. My battery was an Ankor 10,000 and worked well. I only charged my phone to 80% when it was charged from the battery as the last 20% took significantly more power. I turned off most data from apps and all notifications. I also operated on low battery setting and airplane mode when I was using my tracking system. These were recommendations made by Flamingo and a couple of other members of my trail family. I stored all of my electronics and batteries in a Ziplock bag and slept with them to keep them from freezing at night. They do not make for a good pillow.

The map.I used an AWOL Miller's trail guide which was very helpful. Many of my trail family had the Guthooks Trail guide which is the electronic version and allows you to download the trail map and works even if there is no cell signal.

Water filtration. I started with a Katahdin Hiker Pro II but switched to the Sawyer Squeeze to reduce weight. The Katahdin works well but the filters are expensive to replace. It is more complicated with moving parts than the Squeeze. The Squeeze worked well but a word of caution: Do not let the Squeeze freeze. It can crack the porcelain filter and will not filter. You will get water out but it will not be filtered. Also, the Squeeze needs to be backwashed frequently especially if the water source is dirty or has particulates in it. Follow the directions that come with your filter.

Clothing. Wool blend socks worked best for me. They were warm even when they were wet. I would generally wear one for two days and then wash them out and let them dry on the outside of my pack while I wore the other pair. Darn Tough Socks had a great warranty at the time of my hike. They would be replaced for free if they ever had a hole in them. Check the warranty as I have heard it may be changing. Wicking shirts, quick dry hiking pants, and hat were treated with permethrin to reduce the risk of issues with ticks and mosquitos. You can go to duckduckgo.com to research how to do that yourself or have it done professionally. I had long underwear and wool booties to wear at night when the temperature dipped into the teens and single digits. I also learned (the hard way) to keep a set of basic clothes in a dry bag to change into at camp when it was raining so you don't hit the sack in wet clothes. Underwear (optional). Wicking is best.

Sleeping bag. This choice depends on your need for warmth, ability to carry weight, and size you are willing to tolerate. Down bags are generally warmer per weight than synthetic ones but do not hold in the heat when they are wet. The greater fill weight, the warmer the bag. Synthetic bags, while not as warm per ounce of weight, tend to hold more heat in moisture. Down bags need special care when laundering. Regular detergents will significantly reduce the bags longevity if not totally destroy them. Always refer to the manufacturer's guidelines. Drying requires cool temperatures and multiple fluff cycles with tennis balls to drive out the moisture. They should also be stored so they are "fluffed" and not compressed. I have a 700 fill down bag with a liner and on winter excursions take wool socks and fleece booties.

Sleeping pad. When choosing sleeping gear, be sure to seek advice of those who have some experience. My first sleeping pad was called a carrot top due to the bright orange color. It had an insulating factor of

R 3.5 and protected me very well from the cold ground. It was lightweight and fit my body shape well. The drawback with this equipment was that it took seven full breaths to inflate and every time you moved, rolled over, or even just thought about changing positions, it squeaked. Loudly. When I sleep it is more like thrashing, so needless to say, I was always aware that I was a noise machine. No sleeping near enemy territory with this one. This one deflated about halfway through my hike. I used my wife's pad which died about a week later. My new pad is a Sea to Summit and, while a little quieter and lighter, it is not insulating at all. One great feature has a fill bag, which means your lungs are not taxed as much and the interior does not collect moisture and anything else you repeatedly breathe into your bag. It fills with four puffs. I also have a sleeping pad cover (that came in my Cairn package) which reduces noise somewhat and helps to keep the pad cleaner and possibly a little warmer.

Sleeping extras. Sleeping bag liners are a great way to add extra warmth without adding a lot of extra weight. You can improve your sleeping temperature by about fifteen degrees. The other benefit is that it gives your bag a little bit of a barrier from your really dirty, greasy, stanky body. It is usually easier to wash out than your bag. Other things you can add are wool socks or fleece booties. I used a travel sized **My Pillow**. It compresses very well and fits nicely into my stuff sack with the sleeping bag, liner, pad, and pad cover.

Backpack.Make sure you try on a few different packs if possible before you purchase and have someone who knows what they are doing make sure it is adjusted correctly. This is important to have someone help with this because you can't see yourself from the back and side to assess the proper fit. At Neel Gap, my pack was properly adjusted and I am grateful. I did not realize the upper and lower straps to snug the pack to my torso were loose. It felt much more comfortable and stable after those adjustments. If possible, borrow a pack from a friend to try out for a weekend before making a purchase. Be sure all of your stuff fits into the pack and try different configurations as well.

Rain gear. The rain cover for your pack is important as well. The one that came with my pack leaked like a sieve after about the third rain, and that was on the sixth day. It was well used (old) and that was part of the problem. Now I use a $0.99 plastic poncho in warm weather. It is cheap, and covers me and my pack. In the winter or cooler weather, I wear a Patagonia rain jacket but it does not breathe well, so I usually get wetter from sweating than if I didn't wear anything, and then I smell really bad. It does a great job of keeping the wind out and was reasonably priced. I have also worn Frog Toggs, and they do very well at keeping the wing and rain out and are reasonably priced. They are not as durable and the set I had was quite bulky. There are some that are very lightweight, durable and keep the wind and rain out but are out of my budget range.

Tents and other shelter. I have a Big Agnes Copper Spur II because it is relatively lightweight and large enough to fit me and my pack. When hiking with another person, it will fit two persons and has a vestibule on both sides that provides cover from the rain for your pack and shoes. It does not require stakes to hold its shape, so it works well on tent platforms and with rocky tent sites. The drawback for me was the rain fly held water so when it was packed up wet, it was very heavy, adding a couple of pounds to your pack weight. Carbon fiber tents keep the rain out and do not hold moisture and are incredibly light but very expensive. My friend Why Not had one of these tents and used his hiking pole as the center support, and it had to be staked out. It weighed 15 oz. There are other options for shelter. Cowboy camping is done under the stars with no tent at all. His is great if it does not rain and there is no dew in the morning. Hammocks will require two trees, which is usually not a problem on the AT. Some hikers use bivies, which are just like a tarp that keeps the rain and dew off but not necessarily bugs or creatures out.

Nature calling necessities.When nature calls, it is best to be prepared for that trip to the privy or the pine tree, as the case may be. I had a Ziplock bag that had toilet paper, hand sanitizer, my Deuce of

Spades, my trash bag, and just in case things got messy, another Ziplock with baby wipes. At our AT hike orientation, we received instructions, and there are instructions at almost all privies. For the pine tree privy, dig a hole six to eight inches deep and defecate into the hole. Place only biodegradable TP in the hole. Then cover it with leaves and forest debris before covering the hole with dirt. Wet wipes go in your trash bag even if they say biodegradable.

Miscellaneous. I carried a headlamp that was chargeable that I trialed for Cairn. It worked well most of the time, but when it was out of power there was no warning. Lights out. It was a challenge to keep it charged. I usually hit the sack before it got too dark anyway. I also brought my micro-bellows (from Cairn), a small trowel called the Deuce of Spades (from Cairn), a stainless steel spoon knife combo (from Cairn), and a small first aid kit with a variety of Band-Aids, medicines, ointments, and now sewing kit . I carried some really awesome cleats for when I encountered icy conditions on the trail but sent them home the day before I needed them. I made it without falling off a cliff.

Check the warranty and return policy on items before you buy them.

My **OBOZ** hiking boots had a great replacement policy for thru hikers. They replaced the first pair I purchased two times and my second pair once. One of my hiking poles broke and had a one year warranty. Because I purchased it online, they did not honor the replacement warranty. I have not purchased from that national outdoor supply chain since my hike.

11

The Whites

I had lost about twenty-five pounds by the time I reached the White Mountains in New Hampshire. I had no fat pads on the hips or even on the bottoms of my feet. This made walking difficult unless I was wearing my boots. As my pace had slowed, I had great difficulty with some of the climbs in the mountains. I was blessed to have my oldest grandson hike with me for six days, and we tackled the first part of the Whites together. After Lincoln, New Hampshire, I would infrequently connect with my trail family. The weather was great, but the black flies were horrendous. One evening when bending forward to cook a meal for Jacob and myself, my bug netting rode up from the back of my neck and the black flies had a gourmet meal of O Negative. The back of my neck was a mass of bloody welts from the bites. My white t-shirt had blood dripping from it. It was encouraging and a joy to have Jacob hike with me. He arrived at the Post Office in Lincoln, New Hampshire, in the early afternoon on June 6th. My food drop was to be delivered there so it was an ideal place to meet. Some of the Frubble family was planning to stay at Chet's Hostel, and several of the family stayed at a trail angel's condo.

We all gathered at the condo and walked to a nearby bar to grab a bite to eat. Jacob sat between Starfish and Frosting, and I sat towards the end of the table. There were about nine of us there. As the waitress came to clear the plates, Jacob had left two large pieces of bread that were soggy with tomato sauce left on them but he indicated that he was done. Simultaneously, like two starving vultures, Starfish and Frosting said, "Are you not going to eat that?" Jake said, "No, I'm done." They said "Can **we** have it?" Jake shrugged his shoulders and said, "Sure!" Hiker trash displaying hiker hunger. We went for a large ice cream treat before heading to Chet's Hiker Hostel for the evening. The hostel was a garage that had wooden platforms that we could lay our sleeping pad and bag on for the evening. I was able to take a shower and repack after my re-supply. I talked with Chet for quite a while about some of his hiking adventures and personal struggles. We hit the sack at dark thirty as the Whites began in the morning. We hitched a ride with a trail angel to the trail head with most of our trail family. We climbed Mount Moosilauke which was the most physically and mentally intense hike so far on the AT. In five miles we would climb just under 4,000 feet in elevation. We made our way to the Beaver Brook Shelter and had the shelter to ourselves. We made dinner and hit the sack early. The weather was clear. It got down into the low thirties that night, and we woke to frost. We were treated to a spectacular sunrise the next morning of brilliant reds, oranges, lavenders, and blues. I was able to capture the sun as it rose over the mountains illuminating the trees around the shelter and valley below us.

Sunrise view from Beaver Pond Shelter.

Jacob waits for me part of the way up to Moosilauke.

We hiked all day to get to Lonesome Lake Hut. I would highly recommend work-for-stay for thru hikers at the huts when you are going through the Whites. You usually need to get there a little early to get free stay, and it usually allows you to eat any leftovers they have. Our work was to sweep the dining room after dinner and scrub the burners on the stove in exchange for a dinner of leftovers and a spot on the floor in the dining room. Lights are out at nine o'clock, except if you are the Appalachian Mountain Club leaders. Then you can stay in the dining room talking as long as you want to, even until midnight. Jacob was able to sleep through the talking, but I moved out and reclined in my sleeping bag on the porch until they all left and went to their bunks. When they all left the dining room, I gathered my gear and found a spot to sleep in the dining room at midnight. It was a little irritating that the club did not have to follow their own rules. The Appalachian Trail Club is the caretaker of the AT in New Hampshire. They charge a fee to all campers, including thru hikers, to use the campsites or huts.

We were up early before any other hikers were stirring and on our way before breakfast to tackle the Franconian Ridge on our way to Guyot Shelter. We climbed up through the cool forested path and to the ridge as the sun started to warm the trail and us as well. When we stopped for lunch on the ridge at Mount Lafayette, we could see the expanse of the majestic White Mountains and Greenleaf Hut in the distance below us. It was a mile off the trail so we did not descend for a visit but relaxed for a photo op and lunch. We headed up the trail towards Galehead Hut in hopes of scoring some snacks or pastries.

At the Hut, the snacks, pastries, and a little break was welcomed before tackling the climb to South Twin Mountain. After about three-quarters of a mile and 1,000-foot elevation climb, I looked back to see how tiny the hut looked from there. I yelled up to Jake to see where we had been, thinking how small the hut was. He looked off to the south and said, "Wow, Papa, yesterday we were all the way over there," pointing to Mount Lafayette off in the distance. He had a great perspective on the accomplishment of the climb and distance we had travelled. I was impressed with the immediate past 1,000 foot climb over the last three-quarter mile, and he was seeing the extended distance we hiked and climbed in two days. Frequently, during my time hiking I would recommend fellow hikers to stop and look back to see where they had come from. Sometimes you just might see a bear or a moose, and sometimes you may just be encouraged by what you have accomplished and where you have been. I think the same is true for any journey you go on and even in life.

The Guyot Camp Area is where the black flies gorged themselves on my neck. The spot has a tent platform that we had to pay for but it came with coupons for some free food at the huts. There was a great stream of water available to filter just before heading the two tenths mile to the campsite. These camping areas had a central location for cooking so as not to attract bears, rodents, and other creatures from invading spaces where you tent.

As usual, we headed out early the next morning on our way to Ethan Pond for Jake's last night on the trail. The shelter there was empty, and I suggested to Jake that we tent in the shelter if it remained empty. That way, we would be out of the rain and have the protection from mosquitoes and black flies provided by the screen on the tent. It was successful, and we had a good night's sleep before heading out early to the road at Crawford's Notch. It was a rainy, dreary, and cold trek. We would need to travel four miles to a camp store where Jacob would be picked up to return home. When we arrived at the road, I scoured over the trail guide in an attempt to find out what direction we should go to reach the place he would catch the Uber back to Boston for his flight home. Jacob said to me, "Hey, there is a huge dog down the road!" Sure enough, as I turned to look, you could see a moose crossing the road. It does pay to keep your eyes open and look around at the environment as you just might see a moose. Jake and I started to walk on the road towards the grocery camp store four miles up the road where he would catch his ride back to the airport in Boston. I stuck my thumb out to attempt to hitch a ride for our last trail adventure. Several vehicles flew by, but after a short while a small black car stopped and picked us up. It was an older couple, and they shoveled things off the back seats and into the hatch part of the car to make room for us. We introduced ourselves, and I told them we were going to the camp store so Jacob could catch his ride to Boston. We chatted about hiking and general life stuff. They dropped us where I thought the camp store was but, in fact, it was a State Park camp. Unfortunately, it was not open for the season, and it was a mile from where we needed to go. We walked the last mile to the Crawford Notch Camp Store and Campground in a cold drizzly rain. We were pretty wet, cold, and tired and hoping there was some hot food that we might devour when we got there. We were able to order hot sandwiches and perused each aisle carefully looking for the perfect snacks. We were also able to use the bathroom, and it had a flush toilet, running water, and was heated. We were able to connect with the Uber, and she was about an hour away. We snacked and chatted and ate ice cream to pass the time.

Fortunately, the Uber gave me a ride back to the trailhead, and I gave Jake a hug and said goodbye. So, Jake got to see spectacular scenery and a moose, experience hiker trash, staying in a hiker hostel, camping, staying in a shelter, staying in a tent in a shelter (no black flies or mosquitos), camping on a platform, staying in a hut, and hitch hiking with his Papa. Not sure the last one is mamma approved but, I assure you, it was safe.

I felt a bit melancholy as Jake drove away, and I continued north alone again. The weather was cold with blowing rain and a bit scary on some of the open trail near the top. The trail was poorly marked which made it even more of a challenge. I made my way up to the Mizpah Hut and offered to work-for-stay and food which the caretaker gladly offered to me. My work was to inventory and clean out the freezer that was in the basement. Later that evening Why Not came into the hut to warm up but was going to be camping. We talked for a while, and he headed out into the nasty weather to set up his tent and call it a night.

While waiting for dinner to wrap up, I noticed the staff was very busy so I just started doing dishes. The hut leader said I did not need to do that but I persisted and was very much appreciated of my help. After dinner, I did my work task and chowed down on massive leftovers. After eating and finishing up some dinner, a couple came into the hut with their two young children. There were going to be camping but the driving cold rain made the prospect seem pretty miserable. A stay in the hut is very expensive and the couple did not have enough to pay for a stay indoors. As I just had a re-supply of food and cash, and nowhere to spend it anyway, I offered to pay the fee. The manager told me to put my money away, and they would work something out. I was glad they did not have to endure the raging weather outside, especially with two small children.

The next morning, I was up early as usual and I chatted a little with Why Not who came up to the shelter before getting back on the trail. We would hike together every day in the rest of the Whites, southern Maine, and to the summit of Mount Katahdin. We have become good friends.

One of our first challenges was Mount Washington, the highest peak in New Hampshire. It is notorious for high winds and has the highest observed wind speed in the world at 231 MPH. It only has a total of forty days of clear weather each year. The day Why Not and I ascended, it was cold but clear. The previous day had snowy blizzard-like conditions as we read in the journal at Lake of the Clouds Hut where some of my trail family spent a zero due to the weather. When we reached the Lake of the Clouds Hut, we were able to grab a free bowl of leftover oatmeal before heading to the summit about a mile and a half and 1,200 ft climb away. The staff has to pack out any food not eaten so can be very generous with leftovers. You can drive your car up the winding road to get to the top where there is an observatory, a few preserved old buildings, a museum, a restaurant, and a cafeteria. There is a cog railway that goes up and down the mountain and operates on coal. It has been preserved as a part of Mount Washington history. We grabbed some food at the cafeteria and headed down toward Maddison Hut. We had to traverse several snow fields on our way down, and the weather was starting to warm up with the brilliant sunshine. Once past the snow, we could see the hut in the distance. After the hut, the trail was poorly marked and the boulder fields were incredibly difficult and seemed to go on forever. They were almost demoralizing as the fatigue set in.

We did a nero and got a lift to the Rattling River Hostel in Gorham, New Hampshire, for some needed rest and a re-supply. While we were there, we met a section hiker named Pop Tart. He had a car and offered to drive us to Wal Mart and to grab something to eat. The previous year he started a thru hike but had a wedding to attend so was off the trail for a few days for that celebration. While at the rehearsal dinner, he had a massive heart attack and the bride-to-be, who was a cardiac nurse, started CPR and saved his life. He had emergency surgery, and the bride visited him in the hospital the next day after the wedding. He did not return to the trail that year but is determined to complete the adventure. He has a cardiac ejection fraction thirty-nine percent and must listen to and monitor his heart consistently as his life depends on it. He truly hikes his own hike.

On our way out to the trail, I was really bummed out as I discovered my phone charging cord was broken. Pop Tart insisted that I take his as he could just pick one up in his travels. He was and is a trail angel.

There was a section of AT that is notoriously difficult that I have read about in the guide books. It is the Mahousic Notch, a mile long section where you traverse around, over or under house-sized boulders laced with areas of snow and ice left over from the winter. I thought it was a bit difficult but kind of fun like trying to travel through a maze. Many times, the pack would come off to allow you to squeeze through a tiny slot or crawl under a particular boulder. Then pull the pack up behind you or throw it through the tiny passageway before you poke through. It took a lot of energy and the weather started to drizzle a bit towards the end of the notch making things cold and wet. The most challenging part of the trail for me had to be the South Arm of the Mahousic Range. It is a 1,600 foot climb in a little over a mile. Add exhaustion from traversing the Notch, cold blowing rain, the steep sheer face of the arm, and difficult terrain and again it can be demoralizing. I was glad to have Why Not hiking nearby as we were able to encourage each other in this most difficult part so far. I struggled with the steep climbs, and he was challenged with some of the descents. We emerged from the trail to stay at the Hostel of Maine in Stratton, Maine, on the first day of summer. It was a welcome respite and resupply.

12

The Hundred Mile Wilderness

Just the name "Hundred Mile Wilderness" stirs a little anxiety in the back of one's mind. There is a caution sign at the beginning of the Wilderness:

CAUTION

THERE ARE NO PLACES TO OBTAIN SUPPLIES OR GET HELP UNTIL ABOL BRIDGE 100 MILES NORTH. DO NOT ATTEMPT THIS SECTION UNLESS YOU HAVE A MINIMUM OF 10 DAYS SUPPLIES AND ARE FULLY EQUIPPED. THIS IS THE LONGEST WILDERNESS SECTION OF THE ENTIRE A.T. AND ITS DIFFICULTY SHOULD NOT BE UNDERESTIMATED.

GOOD HIKING!

M.A.T.C.

Couple the warning with the descriptions portrayed in many AT guide books, and it sounds formidable. Add some of the tales from those who have experienced it, and it can almost scare you into sweaty palms and dry mouth. After just trudging through the unbelievable challenge of the Whites and mountains of Southern Maine, my anticipation level was elevated to say the least. I had this picture in my mind of fording raging streams, ferocious bears at every turn in the trail and moose lurking around ready to stomp unwary hikers to a pulp. Not to mention the insatiable, bloodthirsty black flies and mosquitos. I tried not to let on to my fear to those I was hiking with, but inside there was fear and trepidation.

There is a rather famous hiker hostel in Monson, Maine, just before you enter the wilderness called Shaw's. The place is run by a young couple, Dude and Hippy Chick, that are avid hikers and understand the mindset of thru hikers. They are great people and very helpful. They have supplies and equipment available for purchase, a great breakfast and a hiker box for items left behind that you are welcome to take for free or you can leave items that you don't need and don't want to carry. They also provide transportation to and from the trailhead as well. Paying for a stay there includes a bed, hot shower, laundry, and options for food close by in town. Why Not and I decided to share a room there and re-supply and recharge before heading out the next morning for the big challenge in my mind.

At Shaw's we met the Blue Crew and to my surprise, most of the Frubble stayed there in the bunkhouse as well. The group included Classic, Flamingo, Starfish, Snow White, Frosting, Physics, Comet, Dr Thunder, Legolas, and Scamper. It was a great reunion and the last time I would see any of my trail family on the AT. We would see the Blue Crew and Fresh Ground there and at Kathadin Stream campground.

That evening, we ate at a restaurant in Monson and purchased a little resupply in town before heading back to Shaw's. We planned out our trek through the Wilderness to let our wives know when and where to expect us. Why Not noticed a sign that indicated we could have a food drop in the Wilderness so we did not have to carry so much food, and we could share the expense. I think it was $40 well spent. It also eased my anxiety significantly. We planned our days as best we could, and I called Gail to let her know when to meet me at

Abol Bridge. We would exit the Wilderness on Tuesday, July second, and summit Katahdin on the third. We planned to hike shorter days through the Wilderness. We scheduled a food drop at Mary Jo Road three days later. We arrived a couple of hours early and had to wait for our supplies. The waiting was horrendous due to the black flies and mosquitoes. I finally set up my tent and took a nap for an hour. That was a wise move so I did not need a blood transfusion before continuing to hike. After the resupply when we got to Potaywadjo Spring Shelter, Why Not did some re-calculations and as we were both tired and both ready to be done, he suggested we do back to back twenty ones and get to Abol Bridge on July first. He emphatically told me, "You are either with me or you are with me!" I guess that means there is only one option. I was absolutely on board, especially since the trail was getting easier the closer to Baxter we hiked.

We hiked with purpose but enjoyed the idyllic Southern Maine scenery. There were multiple crystal clear lakes, beaver ponds, and pristine forests. The smell of hemlock firs and views of the lakes motivated our travel. As we travelled, Why Not spotted a moose on the trail. It appeared to be a juvenile and not very healthy as it wandered slowly along the trail. It did not appear to be aggressive and was very thin. There is a wasting disease that has affected many of the moose in this area.

We shared the trail with a wandering moose.

It was difficult to communicate with the outside world, not only because the cell coverage on the trail was poor in the wilderness but also those waiting for us at the end of the trail had no cell coverage either. Gail had told me that she would travel up a hill near Abol Bridge because it was the only place for many miles where she could get any signal. Sometimes the messages were broken or incomplete or not present at all. She was frustrated and worried that she would miss me on the trail. She was re-assured by Fresh Ground that I would, in fact, emerge from the 100 mile Wilderness on July first at Abol Bridge. Her anxiety level was reduced but still persisted. I was anxious to complete the adventure and missed my sweetheart terribly. I travelled the trail that morning with purpose and determination hoping to see my wife. When I got about a mile from the bridge, I saw Tom a hundred yards ahead of me stop on the trail. As I approached, there it was. A small, fresh, orange colored fruit on the side of the trail told me I was close to the reward. A signature cutie made my heart leap. I almost wanted to run to the end of the trail. Tears of joy came to my eyes as we hugged for several minutes. We then walked the 100 yards to where Fresh Ground had set up his feeding station for thru hikers at Abol Bridge. Tom and I filled our bellies on the gourmet fixins from Fresh Ground. We stopped for ice cream at the Abol Bridge Camp Store before heading toward our last campsite twelve miles from the bridge. Arriving at Katahdin Stream Campground, Gail had already scoped it out and pointed us to the shelter we would be staying and where to register for our final climb.

13

Divert, Avert, or Pervert

(and Other Compromising Events)

My first trail family consisted of Flamingo, Nathan (later known as Classic), and Balto. On one occasion in early March, just before reaching Erwin, the weather was very cold, reaching a frigid thirteen degrees at night. Balto had yet to arrive at the decided upon shelter as nightfall settled with the cold. Flamingo arrived shortly after dark just before everyone else was completing dinner and hitting the sack. Two other hikers, a father and son, arrived shortly after. I had reserved the last available spot in the shelter for Balto as she had said she would be there. The father and son reported they passed her way back and said she would never make it to the shelter that night. They were going to tent anyway as there was not enough room in the shelter for both of them. I assured them that she would indeed make it. Sure enough, she arrived about an hour later. She reported being a bit frustrated in that she had not seen a hiker in four or five hours and stopped on the trail to take a pee. No sooner did she drop her pants when Flamingo came up the trail. Her comment to him was, "You can divert, avert, or pervert." I am not sure what Flamingo decided to do, but he probably averted his attention to another direction. I was glad she was able to share that bit of wisdom for compromising situations on the trail.

Early on in my hike, I saw a lady changing her shirt in the middle of the trail. She did have a sports bra on so I didn't think much of it. As I passed with a friendly greeting of "Have a great Hike!", I noticed that her partner was off the trail about fifty yards visiting the pine tree privy. It was a great time to avert and continue hiking. No stopping to chat at this point. Even in the woods, some people want a little privacy.

While hiking with Comet and her friend, "Tofu Jerky" (She was a vegetarian), I stopped to filter water and grab a snack as they hiked ahead. I hiked north and came over a ridge to catch a glimpse of a bare fanny that was taking care of the call of nature. I immediately diverted my attention and kept on hiking straight. Unfortunately, the trail turned to the right at that place but I continued heading straight and in the wrong direction. I saw several Appalachian Trail Lands signs, but it did not register that there were no white blazes. It only took me a mile or so to realize that I was not on the trail. Argh. My rule is when I realize I am lost; I go back to the last place where I was not lost and figure out where I went wrong to correct the error. Sure enough, where I averted my attention from the trail to avoid being a pervert, I missed the double white blaze indicating the trail turned to the right. By trying not to be the pervert, I got a few extra miles, and I am okay with that. It's a small price to pay for not being a pervert.

Other averting activities were not so taxing on me. In the Whites, I stopped to speak to a young man sitting on a rock at the bottom of a rather steep climb that was just ahead for me. He had just come down and told me he was waiting for his girlfriend who was coming down. About 100 feet up the trail, I saw a young lady working her way down the rather rugged and steep trail. When she was directly above me on the trail, I stepped aside to allow her to come down that part of the trail and told her to come down before I climbed up. As the young lady was coming down, I glanced up to see she was only wearing a hiking skirt. Nothing but the skirt. I averted immediately! I wished her happy hiking. Another averting situation was a time when a young lady at a stealth site a few feet off the trail was applying an ace type wrap around her hips evidently because she had sore pelvic brims from the pack hip belt. That is a common problem which I had for several weeks as well. She had a long sleeved shirt on but her pants pulled down to just above her knees as she was wrapping the large ace bandage around her hips. I did not stop to give her advice about how to avoid the irritation. Avert! At a shelter in the hundred-mile wilderness, I spent the evening at a shelter with a SOBO girl and guy. In chatting in the evening, I found they first met at Katahdin and had become friends over the last few days of hiking. In the morning as I was cooking breakfast in front of the shelter, I noticed she was getting ready for the day's hike south while her hiking friend was still in the sleeping bag as they chatted. Then she removed her top to change her shirt and was wearing nothing underneath. Avert! I never want to be labeled the pervert.

Naked Hiking Day is officially June 21st on the summer equinox. This is not an officially recognized activity in most areas on the trail so you may want to check that out with some of the local hikers or at least be very discreet about it. It is less of an issue if you hike naked with a group, but then you have to ask yourself, "Am I comfortable hiking naked with people?" Many hikers have been known to hike with their pack, boots, and birthday suit. On June 21st in 2019, I was hiking in Maine with Why Not, and it was cold, windy, and drizzling. I hiked fully clothed to the Hostel of Maine. I did get naked on my way to the shower but that was not in public. Maybe some other June 21st when the weather is more conducive to feeling the warm sun refresh the naked body.

At the Laughing Heart Hostel in Hot Springs, North Carolina, I saw a Hiking Naked Calendar. While each month had pictures with full nudity, they were all done so no private parts showed. It was very tasteful. At the end of the calendar there was a request for respectfully done naked hiking pictures for the next calendar. One of our extended family members said she would so love to do that. Not sure if she did or not, and I probably will not get the calendar. I won't ask either as, there again, I don't want to be labeled.

As trail families get more comfortable with their comrades, they will at times, have decreased modesty. Changing clothes is not embarrassing and there is no deference for male or female being present. One of my trail family would at least announce that you may want to avert your eyes as he was changing his underwear. Most of my trail family were relatively discrete in their clothing changes but not necessarily prudish.

Bathing in creeks should always be downstream from where you get your drinking water. After a dreary day of hiking in Virginia and no shower in over a week, I came to a shelter to meet Starfish and Will returning from getting water and having a little creek bath. After dumping my pack, I decided a creek bath would be refreshing and needed. I even had a clean pair of underwear and T-shirt. I headed down the path to the water. It was probably fifty degrees, but I removed my clothes and plunged my feet into the frigid water. The tiny bit of soap and lots of water splashed onto my sinking body was painfully refreshing. I dried off a little with my camp towel and put some clothes on. As I dressed, I noticed a white blaze on a post and realized I took my bath right on the trail. It just goes to show you how important it is to pay attention to your surroundings. Luckily, I did not encounter any other hikers during my bath.

A few tips on pooping in the woods are probably in order at this point. First, you will need to know the rules for the area you are hiking. In many of the Western States, you will need to pack your poop out in a bag because poop does not decompose well in arid regions or high altitudes. In the East and Central States, it is not as important but still there are rules to follow. You will need to dig a cathole six to eight inches deep and 100 feet off the trail and 200 feet away from any water supply. After the deposit fill in with the soil you removed. Sounds easy, right? It is if it is in a farm field, but in the forest, there are roots and rocks and sometimes no soil at all. In those cases, you will need to be a little creative. Clearing out a few rocks and covering the deposit with leaves and then replacing the rocks over the spot and adding a few more for a proper grave covering.

A little advice about the stoop to poop. Don't pull your pants down to your ankles as the geometry of anatomy puts your butt directly over your ankles, and that is where the deposit will land. You will only make that mistake once. Pull your pants down only to above your knees when you straddle the cathole as that is where the poop will land. It may take a little practice, but you will get it eventually. Use biodegradable paper and if you use wet wipes put those in your trash bag as they do not biodegrade. Most of the privies do not have toilet paper, so you will need to bring your own. I always have a small bottle of hand sanitizer, toilet paper, a few baby wipes in a separate Zip-lock, a toilet trash bag, and my Duce of Spades in the top of my pack. The Duce of Spades is a small lightweight digger that is made of aluminum. It is very durable but still lightweight. Some of these skills, you will want to practice. Don't practice in your backyard unless your backyard is in the wilderness and private. But then again, you will have plenty of practice when you are out on the trail.

14

Final Trek to Katahdin

This day was filled with mixed emotions. The strong desire to complete the adventure. The exhaustion that comes with the long distance hike of 2,192 miles and more than 5 million steps can be overwhelming. The elevation change is equal to climbing Mount Everest sixteen times while carrying a thirty pound pack. The rough terrain traversed that had mud, rocks, wet leaves, slippery roots and a variety of other challenging effects. The last part of the trail is reported to be difficult as well. The Hunts Trail that leads to the summit has three distinct sections; the normal AT terrain, the boulder field technical climb, and above the tree line there is a gradual, well marked path to the summit.

The first thing we did was to go to the ranger's station to register for our summit the next morning. The ranger was out, so we returned to the campground shelter. We returned to the campground where Tom set up in the shelter, and I decided that bathing in an ice-cold Katahdin Stream was a better option. Refreshing! Balancing on a rock, I removed most of my disgusting clothing down to my shorts hoping not to plunge into the rushing water. I did a splash bath with a small amount of biodegradable soap. The frigid water felt good on my aching feet after just a minute or two and it was refreshing. The clean clothes were a welcomed addition and probably allowed Gail to let me sleep in Tiny and not gag.

When we returned to see the ranger, I was the thirty-ninth thru hiker to register to summit. The ranger issued us our permit to summit the next day and chatted a bit about our plans for the climb and some issues to be aware of in the area like lightning and hail and torrential rain. We were able to exchange our heavy packs for lighter ones as we would not need a sleeping bag, tent, bear canister, extra clothing, or food. Our day packs had water, snacks, and a rain jacket.

Tom and I devoured a few (most) of Gail's homemade cookies while we planned for our last hike on the AT for this adventure. The weather looked to be unsettled with thunderstorms predicted the next day. We did not want to be on the top of the mountain in a thunderstorm as it is above the tree line and totally exposed. We were up early the next morning with the anticipation of an intense technical climb to the summit. It was a little cool and cloudy but not raining. We started up the Hunts Trail which leads to the summit of Katahdin on July 2nd. The first part of the climb was not unusual or all that strenuous. After passing Katahdin Stream Falls, the climb quickly began to get technical and very strenuous.

Hiking buddy, Why Not as we ascend up the Hunts Trail to Katadhin.

The boulder fields rivaled many of those we encountered in the Whites. The clouds engulfed us, giving the feeling of a cloak of ominous danger as we climbed higher. The next two miles were difficult, and the fog increased as we climbed. There were occasional glimpses of the approaching severe weather. We hoisted ourselves up and around the huge boulders. I appreciated the decreased weight of my pack. Reaching the plateau, the trail flattened and the path was relatively smooth, but we were engulfed in fog with visibility of only twenty-five yards or so. To our relief, the trail was marked very well. To the South, we had no view except for the inside of the clouds that engulfed us but occasionally the clouds would part with a great view to the valley to the North. About a half mile from the summit, the clouds parted briefly and the sun broke through for just a minute. There was no view of the summit from that point but we continued on and the fog quickly engulfed us again. Not being able to see the famous summit plaque engulfed in fog from a distance made the accomplishment of reaching it in the foggy atmosphere emotional. Tom and I took turns taking photos around the sign, and elation flooded over me as I finally reached the climax of an amazing hike.

The summit of Mount Katahdin through the fog.

The weather to the North began to clear, illuminating our climb down the Abol Trail where we would meet our wives to celebrate the completion. We hurried as fast as we safely could down the rocky field as the weather was threatening. After the boulder field, the trail evened out but it started to hail and then lightning. The last half mile, Gail met us with her signature clementines as the thunderstorm delivered torrential rains soaking me to the bone as we walked through a river rushing down the trail. Gail had an umbrella and was only spared a little of the soaking. Our goodbye to Tom was quick as he jumped into his car to head home. Gail and I hurried off to get out of the rain and deposit our soaked bodies into Tiny. We removed the soaked clothes and just sat for a few minutes trying to contemplate the completion of the adventure. The experience of a lifetime was complete.

15

After the Adventure

After the hike was complete, I was shocked to find that my feet and ankles swelled up like balloons. Hiking for four months, eighteen to twenty-five miles a day with a thirty-five pound pack on rugged terrain was no problem but sitting in the van with my feet up, I experienced horrible swelling and pain. I was not expecting that. At this time, I had significant pain in my feet when walking on hard surfaces without shoes. This would last for at least six months.

We spent two nights at Katahdin Stream Campground before heading to Millinocket. Gail and I hiked up to Katahdin Stream Waterfall and enjoyed each other's company at a more leisurely pace. The weather was sunny and warm, somewhat reminiscent of our first visit to the park. We relaxed by the falls to take some pictures. We decided to take our time and visit with Why Not and his wife, Mary, in Boston for a couple of days before heading out for Gail to complete the 14 State Challenge. We would take our time heading south to family in Maryland. As Gail had hiked in most of the states anyway, she only needed to hike some in New Hampshire, Vermont, Massachusetts, New York, and New Jersey. We did a little sightseeing in the quaint little sea port town of Belfast, Maine. We stopped along the way and had several meals of lobster and fish as we were on the east coast which is renowned for its seafood. I did not drive but spent most of the time in the passenger's seat with my feet propped up. When we visited in Boston, we had a great time and enjoyed the hospitality of our friends. We took the ferry from Weymouth to downtown to hike on the Freedom Trail. I was very distracted by the raging hiker hunger that persisted but did enjoy Boston. After hiking the Freedom Trail and enjoying some of the history there, we took the ferry back to Weymouth to Tom and Mary's. Some of their friends had a "Congratulations on Trail Completion" party, and Gail and I were invited to go. Their friends were welcoming and a lot of fun. They gave Tom a plaque that commemorated the trail with a white blaze painted on a small tree slab. Mary got a package that contained some fancy soaps. She smelled them and then as I was standing next to her, asked me what it smelled like. I sniffed at the soap and immediately responded, "A day hiker!" The next morning after a leisurely breakfast, we headed north and west to Hanover, New Hampshire, so Gail could hike from there to Vermont. From there, we stopped at the trailhead that was three miles north of Upper Goose Pond. This was one of my favorite places that Gail really needed to experience. We donned our packs with the bare essentials and headed to the shelter. It is a pretty famous shelter as the volunteer caretaker serves pancakes to the hungry hikers that rest there. We got there early in the afternoon, I showed Gail around the area and we picked out bunks for the evening sleeping quarters. We would share the space with about fifteen other hikers. It was fun chatting about their trail adventures and to provide a little advanced warning about what was to come in their hike. The next morning, I got up early and helped the caretaker brew coffee and make pancakes. We stop cooking when everyone was full. I helped clean up, and then Gail and I took one of the canoes out on the pond to the island for a picnic lunch. We headed back to the van and hiked a bit in Pawling, New York, and followed the trail across the train tracks and on the boardwalk over the wetland. From there, we found the trail in New Jersey and hiked a bit there, completing the last of the states for Gail to complete the 14 State Challenge.

The one challenge I was unable to complete during my hike was the Half Gallon Challenge because I was too early for the park concessions to be open, so we stopped at Pine Grove Furnace State Park in Pennsylvania. As a testament to hiker hunger, in Pine Grove Furnace State Park, there is a Half-Gallon Challenge. The challenge is to consume a half gallon of ice cream in an hour. Many thru hikers try this challenge and some succeed and are rewarded with a coveted small wooden spoon with an inscription that states: "I completed the Half-Gallon Challenge". The selections were few, and I chose raspberry swirl for three pints and chocolate chunk brownie for the last pint. There were several thru hikers hanging out. Gail was there to encourage me for what I thought would slam duck effort. The ice cream shop was closing at 7:00 and we got there at about 6:10. No pressure here. The first three pints were a breeze, but I was full. The last pint went down with significant effort. My stomach had that tight feeling like I couldn't get another bite down. With Gail's encouragement and her pointing out that I only had three minutes until they closed and I would lose my spoon, I forced them down trying not to gag and barf the whole thing up. I completed in fifty minutes and was miserable for at least an hour while Gail drove to our next destination. Then I was hungry again. Hiker hunger raged long after the hike had ended.

We decided to try to make it the hour and a half to my daughter's house instead of stopping for the night. A hot shower, a large dinner, a warm bed, but best of all my daughter, son-in-law, and grandchildren awaited our arrival. We spent a week there, catching up and playing with my grandchildren. I was not ready to get back into hiking mode but my grandkids were excited to get out in the woods with their long haired scraggly looking papa. How could I refuse their enthusiasm? The hiking and playing, although a little painful, was well worth the energy. It was a needed respite and connection time. I will never forget their excitement.

We hit the road very early to head home. We occasionally texted our children to let them know our progress on the journey home. When we got a bit closer, we received a message from our daughter in

LaPorte that her son Owen wanted to carry my pack the last block to our house. When we turned the corner, we saw Owen standing under the stop sign patiently waiting for our arrival. Gail pulled to the side of our street, and I got out of the van and hugged Owen but did not see the rest of the family. We hiked down the block and as we approached our house I saw an exuberant welcoming crowd of friends, family, and neighbors. There were white blazes on the trees in our front yard and on the driveway were chalked welcoming notes resplendent with a path, mountains, and clouds. One chalk note said "Home 0.01 Miles". We were home and I was happy. My daughter Katie also invited friends and neighbors to welcome me home.

My daughter Katie with her children, chalked designs on the driveway and invited friends and neighbors to greet us for our homecoming.

It was a bittersweet time after summit of Katahdin. I knew that I had accomplished my purist of the thru hike of the AT, met some incredible people that will be friends for life, and had an experience unlike any previous experience in my life that few will understand or be able to accomplish. This is something few people get the opportunity to even attempt. I was more than elated to be reunited with my wife and family, who I missed terribly on the trail. It was a challenge to return to my previous lifestyle. Many questions were answered and many more remained. How would life return to normal and really what was normal now?

I was able to share my faith in Jesus Christ, mostly by my actions on the trail, but occasionally in sharing the message of the Gospel. I have learned many things while on the trail to make hiking more fun, safer, faster, or comfortable. I was in awe of the amazing creation we live in. Yes, I believe in a creator. Through evidence, observation, and reasoning I can conclude the evidence does point to a God that loves us and wants the very best live has to offer in this world and the life after our physical death. I am more comfortable sharing the reason I am confident in this world about the life after this one.

On one evening in Massachusetts our trail family had gathered somewhat early in the day. It was dry and comfortable while we sat around chatting at the shelter. Comet was commenting about our trail names and that we all had them and our last name was Frubble and thought that we all needed to have middle trail names because that is more defining to who we are. She said I should have the name "Samaritan Jesus Frubble". I told her that, while I would be honored to have Jesus as my middle trail name, it would be way too lofty of a name to live up to. It was edifying to me that some in my trail family saw Jesus in me. I hope that others on the trail were at least nudged to seek out the difference that Christian faith has made in my life.

The white blaze is the marker that is roughly two inches wide by six inches long and is periodically painted on trees, rocks, posts, roads, guard rails, and other surfaces along the Appalachian Trail. I hope you have as much of an adventure as I did, if you choose to chase it. Happy hiking, and enjoy the addiction!

I was able to share my faith in Jesus Christ, mostly as an example on the trail, but occasionally in sharing the message of the Gospel. I have also had many things while on the trail to make me feel [illegible] uncomfortable. I was in awe of the [illegible] [illegible]

Acknowledgements

Acknowledgements

This book would not be possible without the editing assistance and encouragement from my three daughters, Laura, Julia, and Katie. Laura was especially helpful in suggesting some directional changes and additions. My grandchildren encouraged and supported my adventure in their thoughts and prayers daily. My sister Liz was also very helpful in her initial review and helping me to use proper grammar and spelling. A big thank you also to John Mitchel who encouraged my writing and directed me to Ingram/Spark for self-publishing I also must thank my trail family who encouraged me along the way and we have bonded to become exceptional life-long friends.

The most gratitude must go to my wife Gail, who encouraged and supported me, but also asked the hard questions many of which I failed to even consider. After 50 years she is my rock in this world and I would not have been able to survive the adventure without her. Thank you from the bottom of my heart.

About the Author

Ron Knickrehm is a Christian and semi-retired Physical Therapist. He most of all enjoys his wife and family and church. He enjoys mission work, traveling, gardening, woodworking, canoeing, sailing, camping, backpacking, and generally the outdoors. He is an avid runner and runs regularly with a group called the Ogres (Old Guys Running Every Sunday). He has been married to his high school sweetheart for 50 years. He served in the US Army for two years and was stationed in Germany most of that time. He presently serves on the LaPorte County Park Board and enjoys speaking to groups about hiking and backpacking. He can be contacted at ATSamaritan2019@gmail.com to talk about backpacking or present to a group interested in learning more about the adventure.

www.ingramcontent.com/pod-product-compliance
Ingram Content Group UK Ltd.
Pitfield, Milton Keynes, MK11 3LW, UK
UKHW021838270726
14058UKWH00002B/229

9 798218 055356